Soil & Roots

Cultivating Deep Discipleship

Brian Fisher

SOIL & ROOTS

Copyright © 2024 by Brian Fisher

All rights reserved.

Unless otherwise noted, all scripture quotations taken from the (NASB®) New American Standard Bible®, Copyright © 1995 by The Lockman Foundation. Used by permission. All rights reserved. lockman.org

No part of this book may be reproduced in any form or by any electronic or mechanical means, including information storage and retrieval systems, without written permission from the author, except for the use of brief quotations in a book review.

Contents

Acknowledgments

A book is always a group effort, even if only one person's name makes it to the front cover.

Dr. Tim Boswell has been my faithful and stalwart editor, chief critic (in the best sense of the word), and intellectual sparring partner on the last several book projects. Once again, his sterling contributions shine brightly.

Soil & Roots exists today for numerous reasons, but a primary one is the strong and consistent encouragement of Kyle Moody, now co-host of the *Soil & Roots* podcast. And his good-natured tolerance of my constant harassment is much appreciated.

Marc Ridout has been a source of hope, brotherhood, and support for many years. Thanks to him and Amanda for allowing us to work much of this out at their lake house.

I'm indebted to Matt Davis for his profoundly important thoughts and insights regarding the mission and vision of Soil & Roots, which seeped into the fabric of this book.

Several kind people from our Greenhouse also agreed to read and critique an early draft. Thanks to Amanda Ridout, Lori Wood, and Dr. Chris and Elaine Russo.

Knowing that not everyone would universally resonate with the ideas in the book, I asked a few of my friends from the Colson Center Fellows program to take a weed-whacker to it, and they gratefully agreed. Special thanks to Austin Arabie, Nathan Young, and Chip Schmidt for their comments and perspectives.

A number of other pastors and friends agreed to meet with me over breakfasts, lunches, and video calls to hash out and wrestle with the themes and concepts contained herein. Thanks to Patrick Poteet, Luke Post, Jim Reiter, Adam Ormord, Bill Burns, Jason Miller, and Ron Quiditano.

To Zach Leighton, Sarah Van Winkle, and the rest of the team at Reliant Creative: you crushed it.

Writing a manuscript is only half the battle. Crafting it into a book to hold in our hands or read digitally is another thing entirely. My gratitude to Allison Ulloa and Jessica Glasner for getting this over the finish line.

I'm particularly grateful to the group of families who agreed to form the very first Greenhouse and whose input and contributions have made the journey all the richer: the Moodys, Woods, Ridouts, and Russos.

Our sons, Caleb and Zach, provided inspiration for the book by forming their own "Greenhouse" of young men, journeying together to become more like Jesus.

My wife, Jessica, will always be my dearest and best friend, closest confidante, ardent supporter, and fellow risk-taker. There is no book and no ministry without her.

Duc In Altum

Introduction

Several years ago, my wife, Jessica, and I were forced out of a dynamic Christian non-profit ministry that I had co-founded. No accusations or explanations were offered. We were stunned, confused, and dismayed. The organization has continued successfully doing the work for which it was intended, just without us.

It's common in these types of awkward situations for relationships to become strained or disappear altogether. Most of our friendships, some of which were more than twenty years old, ended overnight. People we had known and loved vanished. It was like we had died.

We lost our careers, our calling, and our community. In the blink of an eye, I had gone from a successful leader, seasoned executive, sought-after speaker, and Christian thought leader to a disillusioned, devastated, exhausted nobody.

I hastily started a new company, attempting to continue the type of work that was so personally meaningful to me, work to which I was sure God had called me.

It failed within four months.

Inevitably, the depression came, what St. John of the Cross referred to as "the dark night of the soul."[1]

I condemned myself to a prison of isolation. What kind of

Christian leader is removed from the organization he started? How could I have been so terribly disillusioned and self-deceived?

I withdrew into an inner sanctum of doubt, confusion, relentless self-introspection, and a growing sense of disenchantment with the Christian institutions, systems, communities, friendships, and beliefs I had held so dear. They had failed. Or I had failed them. I wasn't sure.

There were nights I couldn't sleep and days when that was all I wanted to do. I lost weight. Jessica became concerned about my health and safety.

We kept going to church, but our church was growing so fast that few people knew anyone there. It seemed the point of the church was to go to a Sunday event, sing a few songs, hear an entertaining and slightly provoking sermon, give money, and leave as fast as you came. The church was far more concerned about bottoms in seats than in any one person's journey or struggle.

In fact, the traditional Christian rituals and relationships I had relied on for so long now seemed empty or shallow. Maybe even fake.

Bible verses I had long ago memorized seemed to fail.

> Trust in the Lord with all your heart and do not lean on your own understanding. In all your ways acknowledge Him, and He will make your paths straight.[2]

I thought I had trusted God with my whole heart, and yet the last phrase I would use to describe this new, dismantled stage of life was "straight paths."

> If you abide in Me, and My words abide in you, ask whatever you wish, and it will be done for you.[3]

I had apparently not been abiding in Jesus because most of what we had asked for had just crumbled to the ground.

> Be anxious for nothing, but in everything by prayer and supplication with thanksgiving let your requests be made known to God. And the peace of God, which surpasses all comprehension, will guard your hearts and your minds in Christ Jesus.[4]

In light of our loss, how were we supposed to be "anxious for nothing"? And where was this elusive "peace that passes all understanding"?

It wasn't just that our world had been thrown into chaos. It was that my response to the tumult didn't reflect the type of character that the Bible paints as a mature follower of Jesus. I thought I had been walking with Jesus since I was six years old. Where were all the "abiding," "peace," and "contentment" that are so often depicted as character traits of a long-term, mature Christian?

Surely, there was more to the Christian experience than a weekly service, routine Bible study, and volunteerism. I had done all those things my entire life. Where had they gotten us?

No, I was missing something on my journey with Jesus. Something deeper. Something more sustaining than the practices and rituals that had held me up so far. I was sure that I was a Christian. I just wasn't sure I was a disciple, someone who was supposed to be intimately resting in Jesus's easy yoke.

Not finding any other path out of the ever-increasing darkness, I finally agreed to speak with a counselor. I wasn't thrilled about it. Though I respected the counseling profession, I thought it was for people who rarely opened their Bibles, came from abusive homes, or had serious marriage problems. None of those described me.

Around the same time, I came across a book called *Renovation of the Heart* by philosopher and theologian Dallas Willard.[5] I didn't know who he was, but I figured if anyone's heart needed renovating, it was mine. He used phrases such as "spiritual formation" and "ideas and images" that were new to me. And he wrote with a kindness that took me aback.

So began a slow, painful, sometimes halting, yet comprehensive journey of exploration and healing, a journey with both a counselor and with what had always been close friends of mine: books.

I started reading Willard and then ventured into dozens of other texts, ranging from ancient church history to anthropology, neuroscience, philosophy, spiritual disciplines, trauma recovery, the history of Western thought, theology, and cultural studies.

Throughout, several questions drove me: What was the "more" I was missing in my life with Jesus?

And I wanted to know what happened to our own community. Why were we deeply loved and highly valued when we were useful, popular, and powerful, but rejected and abandoned as soon as our usefulness dried up? If being in a Christian community implied a steadfast commitment to each other through times of trial and despite faults or weaknesses, why had our community failed? Why had we failed?

And I wanted to know if I was alone and unique in this journey. Was there anyone else out there struggling with betrayal, abandonment, deep questions, new doubts, and a sense there was far more to the Christian life than a prayer of salvation, Bible studies, worship services, and mission trips?

Was anyone else questioning whether the way Christianity is currently manifested in many institutions actually resembles what the first Christians modeled and experienced? Was anyone else curious about whether our ideas regarding "discipleship" really match up with what Jesus meant when He used that term?

The Bible makes seemingly impossible promises and claims about a disciple's life of patience, effective prayer and serenity, even when faced with anxiety and fear—a life of abundance, selflessness, and peace, particularly in the midst of trials and suffering.

I realized I had dozens of "micro" questions—about myself, our family, our community, and our story. And I had dozens of "macro" questions—about modern discipleship, our churches, and our culture.

As a means of working out both kinds of questions, I started a small podcast called *Soil & Roots*. It was and continues to be a place to explore our stories, the story of Jesus, the modern-day church, and the state of our culture.

As the audience and I delved into deep and provocative themes and ideas related to discipleship, a few people started raising their hands, asking their own questions, and sharing their reflections.

"I'm coming to believe there's more to the Christian life than what I thought."

"I've been in the church my entire life and didn't know what a disciple really was."

"I didn't realize I had permission to explore my personal story and how it impacts my relationship with God, myself, and other people."

"I am terribly lonely sitting in church. Where can I find people who just want to be with me?"

A group of us—friends with an interest in these ideas—met and prayed about Soil & Roots, and we concluded it was more than a podcast. It's an opportunity to recapture ancient ideas and rhythms that have largely been lost in modern Christianity, yet are of vital importance to experiencing the depths of genuine discipleship and the abundant life found in Christ. Because of this, it's also an opportunity to connect, heal, redeem, integrate, and find hope.

It's a means to address what Dallas Willard called "the Great Omission"—the irony that the modern church routinely preaches about making disciples but struggles to do it.

Soil & Roots: Cultivating Deep Discipleship digs into some areas of our spiritual journey not normally addressed in our Christian institutions. It asks questions of our faith, our stories, our church, our culture, and our hearts that dive below our normal rituals and rhythms. *Duc In Altum*... put out into the deep.

In many ways, this book is a "primer" for those of you interested in a deeper spiritual walk, perhaps peeking into your own story, or for those of you yearning for an immersive community that, for many of us, has remained elusive.

Because the team at Soil & Roots firmly believes that the journey of our hearts, churches, and culture is best explored and experienced in intentional small gatherings, you'll also find guidance, ideas, and next steps for forming or joining this type of community, which we call Greenhouses. In Chapter 10, we'll outline this type of community and how you might form or join one.

You may be currently experiencing a dark night of the soul, or perhaps you've experienced several. You may have doubts, questions, longings, and frustrations that remain unexpressed because much of modern Christianity often doesn't allow such expression. You may be wondering if there is far more to the Christian life than what most of us experience. Perhaps in your heart of hearts, you sense a disconnection between you and God, you and others, or perhaps between you and yourself.

Be of good hope. There is more. The Christian life is one best experienced in an intentional community, one that allows for the exploration of our stories and others' stories, that asks how we fit into the grand narrative of human history found in the Bible. This community is a place where doubts and questions are welcomed, where patience and kindness are extended, where there is more resting than doing, more thoughtfulness than action, and a recognition that God not only loves you, but He also likes you.

If Dallas Willard is right, that modern Christianity is suffering from the Great Omission, may this book be a starting point for our community journey into the deep end of discipleship, and may that lead to individual, family, church, and cultural healing and redemption.

Brian Fisher
Founder, Soil & Roots

---

1. Father Richard Conlin, "Summary of The Dark Night of the Soul by St. John of the Cross," *The Prodigal Catholic Blog*, accessed October 18, 2023, https://prodigalcatholic.com/2019/05/31/summary-of-the-dark-night-of-the-soul-by-st-john-of-the-cross/.
2. Proverbs 3:5–6
3. John 15:7
4. Philippians 4:6–7
5. Willard, D. (2021). *Renovation of the Heart.* NavPress.

Part One
Deep Discipleship

One
The Disconnected Disciple

We are half-hearted creatures, fooling about with drink and sex and ambition when infinite joy is offered us, like an ignorant child who wants to go on making mud pies in a slum because he cannot imagine what is meant by the offer of a holiday at the sea. We are far too easily pleased.

—C. S. Lewis [1]

Disconnected

Many people in the West have the sense of being lonely, isolated, and disconnected from God, other people, themselves, and creation. Certainly, this is true for many people who aren't following Jesus, but it's also true for many who do. Others feel connected to God, yet experience a hunger or longing for a fuller, richer experience of our faith. Our church life may be meaningful, but many of us are wondering if there is something more to the spiritual life than a weekly worship event, some private devotions, and a Bible study, something deeper, something intangible.

The Bible certainly alludes to a deeper, more secure, more stable kind of life when it talks about the peace that exceeds our understanding, abiding with God, the abundant life, joy amid suffering, unity among our friends and family, conquering sin, and a life-changing love for God, our self, and our neighbor.[2] It describes a life where we genuinely love our enemies and can overcome anger, anxiety, and fear.

Perhaps we feel a disconnection in our prayer life. We're told to pray, and we appreciate the privilege of prayer, yet we don't seem to grasp the experience and effectiveness of the prayer life promised in the Bible.

> When we examine ourselves, all too often we discover that our praying does not rise to the demands of the situation, being so limited that it is little more than an oasis amid the waste and desert of the world's sin. Recall the words of our Lord: "Most assuredly, I say to you, he who believes in Me, the works that I do he will do also; and greater works than these he will do, because I go to My Father" (John 14:12). Who of us, in praying, measures up to this awesome promise?
>
> —E.M. Bounds[3]

Indeed, do I measure up to this promise? Is my life characterized by doing "greater works" than when Jesus walked the earth?

The Bible describes the life of a disciple as so... free... but that freedom seems hard to grasp.

Do I deeply sense God's presence? Can I truly conquer lifelong, habitual sins? Can I envision a life where fear and anxiety are calmly and powerfully acknowledged and worked through?

This type of life sounds like a fantasy or like service in some monastery compared to the lives we often lead.

We tend to cover up the underlying sense that there's more to the Christian life with the innumerable distractions available to us today:

busyness, leisure, eating, exercise, running our kids around, and even our church activities. In darker periods, we may struggle with various addictions, even the socially acceptable ones.

But the yearning in our hearts persists. We long to know and be known. We ache for the intimacy, power, comfort, security, and freedom promised in the Bible. These qualities are supposed to characterize the life of a mature disciple of Jesus.

Yet our relational distance, confusion, irritation, anxiety, anger, and restlessness remain. Perhaps it's because we've misunderstood or distorted Jesus's command to make disciples. To this, Dallas Willard wrote:

> But in place of Christ's plan, historical drift has substituted "Make converts [to a particular 'faith and practice'] and baptize them into church membership." This causes two great omissions from the Great Commission to stand out. Most important, we start by omitting the making of disciples and enrolling people as Christ's students, when we should let all else wait for that. Then we also omit, of necessity, the step of taking our converts through training that will bring them ever-increasingly to do what Jesus directed.[4]

Is Christianity in the West, with its innumerable churches, organizations, ministries, and teaching, suffering from a plague of disciple-less communities and, therefore, a lack of people who have a deep, abiding, peaceful relationship with God, others, and themselves?

Three Key Questions

If you've spent any length of time in a church, you've heard the word "disciple" hundreds if not thousands of times. It's one of those words that, because we've heard it so often, its meaning becomes cloudy and confused under layers of stories, sermons, Bible studies, articles, podcasts, and videos.

Yet making disciples is at the heart of what's known as the Great Commission:

> And Jesus came up and spoke to them, saying, "All authority has been given to Me in heaven and on earth. Go therefore and make disciples of all the nations, baptizing them in the name of the Father and the Son and the Holy Spirit, teaching them to observe all that I commanded you; and lo, I am with you always, even to the end of the age."[5]

Since this is the last thing Jesus told His followers before His ascension, we should take special note. Jesus came and incepted His kingdom, and He instructed His followers to continue His work by making disciples of the nations. In Mark's version, Jesus says we are to share this good news with the entire earth.

> And He said to them, "Go into all the world and preach the gospel to all creation. He who has believed and has been baptized shall be saved; but he who has disbelieved shall be condemned. These signs will accompany those who have believed: in My name they will cast out demons, they will speak with new tongues; they will pick up serpents, and if they drink any deadly poison, it will not hurt them; they will lay hands on the sick, and they will recover."[6]

If discipleship is such a central aspect of Christianity, it's worth exploring some key questions.

1. *What is a disciple?*
2. *Why should we make disciples?*
3. *How are disciples made?*

We'll explore the first two questions in this chapter and dive into how disciples are made in the next.

What is a Disciple?

A simple, succinct definition suggested by various theologians is "an apprentice of Jesus."

An apprentice is:

- one bound by indenture to serve another for a prescribed period with a view to learning an art or trade
- "one who is learning by practical experience under skilled workers a trade, art, or calling (a carpenter's *apprentice*)"[7]

Another definition states:

- "The word *apprenticeship* comes from the Old French *aprentiz* meaning 'someone learning' and the Anglian suffix *-skip*, meaning 'state, condition of being.' An apprenticeship is when someone is in a state or condition of learning from a master in a field."[8]

That sums up a "disciple" quite succinctly—someone who follows a master and is in a state or condition of continually learning from that master.

In modern evangelicalism, the term "disciple" is often and incorrectly used interchangeably with the term "convert," as Willard noted above. A convert is simply someone who has had a change of mind or heart. But a disciple is engaged in a lifelong state of apprenticeship.

Why Should We Make Disciples?

To explore the reasons why we become and make disciples, we first need to explore some ideas about anthropology or what it means to be human.

In our current age, we tend to make certain assumptions about discipleship. For example, some assume that a disciple is a person accumulating knowledge about Jesus and the Bible, who knows a lot of Scripture, shows up at church each week, attends regular Bible study, and so on. But, as we're about to discover, the reason we become and make disciples concerns not so much a journey of the head as of the heart.

What it Means to be Human

Singer, songwriter, and poet Rich Mullins wrote a song called "Higher Education and the Book of Love," and it opens with a critical question and his response:

> What does it mean to be human?... I cannot help but believe that it means we are spiritual—that we are responsible and that we are free—that we are responsible to be free.[9]

Philosopher James K. A. Smith explored the same question, though he asked it in a slightly different manner.

Are human beings primarily *thinkers*, *believers*, or *desirers*?

Smith's claim is that modern Christianity consciously or unconsciously assumes that humans are primarily thinkers and that our formation is primarily accomplished through the intake of information. But he proposes that "formation" and "information" are not the same.

> If we consider these two very different understandings of education (the informative and the formative), and the different understandings of the human person that are at work behind them, I suggest that, over the past decades, institutions of Christian education have unwittingly absorbed the former and eschewed the latter. Many Christian schools, colleges, and universities—particularly in the Protestant tradition—have taken on board a picture of the human person that owes more to modernity and the Enlightenment than it does to the holistic, biblical vision of a human person.[10]

A pastor friend of mine calls this the "brains on a stick" assumption. It's the idea that humans are primarily formed through accepting pieces of information, through instruction.

Smith isn't alone. Numerous contemporary authors have voiced concerns that the modern church has unwittingly prioritized Descartes's position of "I think therefore I am." The fear is that the highly rational and intellectual Enlightenment and Age of Reason have worked their way into the fabric of modern Christianity, producing Christians who may be able to verbally express correct Christian positions or doctrines and yet are no more loving or wise or compassionate than anyone else.

Dallas Willard most likely would have agreed with Smith. He concluded that the words "heart," "spirit," and "will" in the Bible are essentially synonyms. They all refer to the core of who we are. And Willard described how true formation is the work not only of the brain but of the heart.

This isn't to discount or minimize the role of the mind (or the body). Yet if the very root of our being, our identity, is our heart, our spirit, then that has enormous implications for how we live. And it has enormous implications for the reasons we become and make disciples.

Perhaps Rich Mullins was right: to be human is to be spiritual or "of the heart." God is Spirit, and each of us is an embodied spirit. God is love, and He has given us the capacity to love from our hearts—from our spirits.

This also suggests that James K. A. Smith is correct: we are not primarily thinkers. Shockingly, we are not even primarily believers. We are primarily desirers. We are lovers.

Spiritual Formation

If a disciple is an apprentice of Jesus, we are now presented with a far deeper, more intimate answer to the question of "Why should we be a disciple and make others?"

We apprentice with Jesus for the purpose of our hearts being formed more like His.

Being a disciple is certainly about the mind—about learning, studying, listening—and yet it's more than that. It's about the very bedrock of who we are, our hearts, being formed increasingly into the image of the heart of Jesus.

It's about "heart formation." And, if we accept the premise that "heart" and "spirit" tend to be synonyms, we may use the term "spiritual formation." Or we may even say "character formation."

What does it mean to have our spirits formed to be more like our Master in our lifelong apprenticeship? It means that, over time, we love what He loves. We desire what He desires, so we do the things He does.

Human beings desire all sorts of things, though modern science has shed some light on our deepest, core yearnings.

Christian counselor Adam Young paraphrases neuroscientist Curt Thompson, who claims that "when each one of us comes into this world, we enter it looking for someone looking for us. Our deepest desire and highest hope is that there will be someone looking for us, and that this person will always be there for us and will pursue our hearts with a genuine desire to truly know us."[11]

These comments are worth our contemplation. The deepest human desire in the deepest part of who we are is to be known and to know that the person who knows us will be there for us.

We're now beginning to sense that the answer to "Why do we become and make disciples?" isn't just about Christian rituals, study, evangelism, and duty. It's about the formation of our hearts through our deepest desire being met—the desire to know and be known—and then inviting others into this type of deep, abiding, experiential relationship.

If discipleship now sounds a bit like falling in love and deepening that love over time, we're on the right track.

If you've fallen in love, chances are it wasn't because of the information you shared with your lover. My wife didn't fall in love with me because I told her my name, my birthday, my social security number, and my hobbies. There are more profound things at play when we fall in love, things that mature and flourish over time.

Love isn't just facts. It's the intangible, rooted, unspoken, emotional entangling of ourselves with another person.

Likewise, spiritual formation involves the concept of "withness." It is about being *with* someone—experiencing them. Sometimes, that means words and facts, but much of the time, it means things far deeper than spoken words can express.

This "withness" may not be a concept we're used to exploring when learning about discipleship. Yet God is so intent on being "with" us that He arrived in person in the form of Jesus and now dwells with us in the person of the Holy Spirit. Where does the Holy Spirit reside in us? In our hearts, our spirits. We might also call this our "roots."

It's as if the very heart of God is entangled with our hearts. It's as if His roots are intimately intertwined with our roots. If you have ever questioned whether God loves you, may I suggest that there is no other entity in the history of the universe that loves you so much that His heart is wrapped around your heart.

He is Immanuel, God with us. God in us. God's perfect, pure roots are lovingly entangled with our calloused, dirty roots.

The imagery may make us a bit uncomfortable because it is so raw, so intimate. Yet God unabashedly loves us and desires to be with us. He passionately pursues us to fulfill what Curt Thompson claims is our deepest desire: to be known by someone who will always be there for us.

The Bible explores the concept of the heart and spirit as our center, our core, and it unashamedly proclaims the love of God. He wants our hearts. He wants the very depths of who we are.

Delight yourself in the Lord; And He will give you the desires of your heart.[12]

You will seek Me and find Me when you search for Me with all your heart.[13]

Create in me a clean heart, O God, and renew a steadfast spirit within me.[14]

...and hope does not disappoint, because the love of God has been poured out within our hearts through the Holy Spirit who was given to us.[15]

Now He who establishes us with you in Christ and anointed us is God, who also sealed us and gave us the Spirit in our hearts as a pledge.[16]

Because you are sons, God has sent forth the Spirit of His Son into our hearts, crying, 'Abba! Father!'[17]

A disciple is an apprentice of Jesus, someone who centers their life around learning from their master, someone who gives up their way of doing things in favor of the master's way of doing things.

And the reason *why* we become disciples is now clear: to actually become more like our master. It isn't simply to know more; it's to take on the characteristics of the person we're serving. To love like Jesus loves, to desire what He desires, to do what He does.

Not only are our spirits to be formed more like His, but we are also to make other disciples whose spirits are being formed more like His.

This is the Great Commission: to pour ourselves into the lives of others who desire to have their hearts transformed into the likeness of the King of the Cosmos.

Chapter 1 Key Takeaways

1. We often experience a disconnection from God, others, ourselves, and creation. Though the Bible makes various promises about a deep and abiding life, we often struggle to live that kind of life.
2. A primary reason for this struggle is that the West suffers from a lack of genuine discipleship, a struggle to make people who live and love like Jesus.
3. A disciple is an apprentice of Jesus, someone who continually learns from Him and grows to become more like Him.
4. Human beings are not primarily thinkers or even believers. We are primarily desirers or lovers, and our greatest desire is to be known and to know the person who knows us will be there for us.
5. To that end, we become disciples in order for our hearts to be formed more like Jesus, to love as He loves, think as He thinks, and relate as He relates. This is why discipleship is

often referred to as "spiritual formation" or "character formation."

---

1. Lewis, C. S. (1949). *The Weight of Glory* (First American Edition), (p. 2). Macmillan Press.
2. Philippians 4:7
3. Bounds, E. M. compiled by Sorenson, S. W. (2006). *The Best of E.M. Bounds* (p. 81). Honor Books.
4. Willard, D. (2014). *The Great Omission: Reclaiming Jesus's Essential Teachings on Discipleship* (pp. 5–6). HarperCollins. Kindle Edition.
5. Matthew 28:18–20
6. Mark 16:15–18
7. "Apprentice," *Merriam Webster*, accessed October 31, 2023, https://www.merriam-webster.com/dictionary/apprentice#:~:text=a,a%20carpenter's%20apprentice.
8. "Apprenticeship," *Vocabulary.com*, accessed October 19, 2023, https://www.vocabulary.com/dictionary/apprenticeship#:~:text=The%20word%20apprenticeship%20comes%20from,a%20master%20in%20a%20field.
9. Rich Mullins, "Higher Education and the Book of Love," *Genius*, accessed October 19, 2023, https://genius.com/Rich-mullins-higher-education-and-the-book-of-love-lyrics.
10. Smith, J. K. A. (2009). *Desiring the Kingdom: Worship, Worldview, and Cultural Formation* (p. 31). Baker Academic.
11. Adam Young, "Attachment: What It Is and Why It Matters," *Adam Young Counseling*, accessed October 19, 2023, https://adamyoungcounseling.com/free-documents/.
12. Psalm 37:4
13. Jeremiah 29:13
14. Psalm 51:10
15. Romans 5:5
16. 2 Corinthians 1:21–22
17. Galatians 4:6

Two
The Surprising Discipleship Journey

> We truly live at the mercy of our ideas; this is never more true than with our ideas about God.
>
> —Dallas Willard[1]

We've answered our first two questions: what is a disciple, and why do we make them? A disciple is an apprentice of Jesus for the purpose of becoming more like Him. This is spiritual formation, an ongoing journey of our hearts slowly transforming into His heart.

We now come to our third question. How does this happen? How do our spirits truly become formed more like the spirit of our King? How does this discipleship journey move forward?

The Critical Journey

In my quest to answer this question, I came across several thinkers and authors who attempted to describe our discipleship journey in various stages. Though several models describe spiritual formation, one, in particular, was helpful to me as I wrestled with Willard's "Great

Omission"—the irony that the modern church routinely preaches about making disciples but rarely does it.

In the late 1980s, Janet Hagberg and Robert Guelich wrote a book titled *The Critical Journey*, in which they theorized that our journey with God can be described in six stages. It's not that we necessarily move through these stages in a straight line. We may bounce in between a few or skip one or two. We may spend years in just one stage, perhaps getting stuck there for a period of time or for the rest of our lives.

Stage 1 is a **Recognition of God**. This is when we become aware of God, or perhaps when we choose to follow Jesus.

The authors titled Stage 2 the **Life of Discipleship**. We come to know God, and then we take time to learn more about Him. This stage entails activities like Bible studies, lectures, classes, and perhaps being mentored. It's characterized by a deep desire to know more about this God to whom we've just been introduced.

However, I'll call this stage the **Life of Learning**. With due respect to the authors, for our purpose, "discipleship" encompasses all six stages.

Stage 3 is the **Productive Life**. This is when we start to give back. We begin to serve. Perhaps we volunteer at church, work in the nursery, mentor others, or serve on mission trips. We know God, we know more about God, and now we're ready to share God with others through a myriad of opportunities.

I suspect most of us recognize these three phases and have spent time in each. Many of our stories involve us coming to Christ, joining a community of faith, learning more about Him, and then taking on a serving role in some capacity.

Before I reviewed Hagberg and Guelich's book, I was unaware that phases might exist beyond these first three. I thought the first set of three were all there was.

I was very wrong.

Stage 4 is called the **Journey Inward**.

> It almost always comes as an unsettling experience yet results in healing for those who continue through it. Until now, our journey has had an external dimension to it. Our life of faith was more visible, more outwardly oriented, even though things certainly were happening inside us.
>
> At this stage, we face abrupt change to almost the opposite mode. It's a mode of questioning, exploring, falling apart, doubting, dancing around the real issues, sinking in uncertainty, and indulging in self-centeredness.[2]

Somewhere in Stage 4, we come across **"the Wall."** As I mentioned in the introduction, St. John of the Cross called this type of experience the "dark night of the soul."

> The Wall represents the place where another layer of transformation occurs, and a renewed life of faith begins for those who feel called and have the courage to move into it... This experience is perhaps the most poignant example of mystery in the whole journey of faith... Experiencing the wall is both frightening and unpredictable.[3]

They cited some biblical examples of the Wall: Jonah in the belly of the whale, Job in the middle of his illness, Elijah when he hid in the cave from Jezebel, Sarah being barren for so long and finally giving up and giving Hagar to her husband.

The Wall is often brought on by some sort of crisis: a job loss, a cancer diagnosis, a death in the family, divorce, betrayal, a move, wondering if our career or our ministry or our perspective is valid or "right."

When we hit the Wall, we have a few options. We may press into it and engage in the struggle and introspection it brings. Or we may turn back and settle into a previous stage because we just aren't willing to dig beneath the surface. In some cases, a person simply abandons the faith altogether... they "deconstruct."

As I began to explore my own story in the midst of the crisis I described earlier, it was clear I had stumbled into Stage 4 and the Wall. It wasn't the first time, though the last time I had ignored the Wall, turned around, and made sure to keep my life so busy and chaotic that I wouldn't have to think about it.

However, the Wall is a pivotal part of our journey because it often causes us to revisit the truths and ideas we assumed when we were younger. And we discover God in new ways. We experience Him more deeply, and that draws us into a more trusting relationship with Him. We learn to surrender.

After the Wall comes Stage 5, which is the **Journey Outward**. Our attention shifts from exploring and discerning our own stories to exploring and discerning others' stories. Healing is taking place in the bedrock of our hearts, and we begin to experience a more profound sense of compassion, empathy, and goodness for others.

Last comes Stage 6, **A Life of Love**.

> At this stage we reflect God to others in the world more clearly and consistently than we ever thought possible... When we are at stage 6, we have lost ourselves in the equation, and at the same time we have truly found ourselves. We are selfless. This factor allows us to do the most extraordinary things. We may figuratively wash other people's feet or give our very lives in the service of God... We are at peace with ourselves, fully conscious of being the person God has created us to be. Obedience comes very naturally without deliberation because we are so immersed in God's work.[4]

The authors list other characteristics: wisdom gained from life's struggles, compassionate living for others, including our enemies, detachment from things and stress. They make the case that someone living in Stage 6 may appear strange to the rest of us.

Someone in this last stage isn't trying to perform or accumulate much of anything. They may appear slow. They're so unconcerned with things that concern us, we aren't sure quite what to do with them.

Truly selfless? At peace with ourselves? Genuinely loving our enemies? A life that calmly acknowledges and alleviates anger, anxiety, and fear? Strange indeed.

As I re-read their descriptions of disciples in Stages 5 and 6, I realized they were articulating a Christian life with which I was largely unfamiliar. However (and not surprisingly), their descriptions seemed to align with the abiding promises and principles found in the Bible regarding mature disciples.

Hagberg and Guelich were describing the life of someone who was truly becoming more like Jesus—not just someone who knew a lot about Him, but someone whose character was being formed like His.

However, they made a somewhat startling claim: the institutional church is almost exclusively concerned with Stages 1-3. Very few people have access to churches or communities to help guide us into the later stages of the spiritual journey. The reasons why this problem exists may well be the subject of other books, but suffice it to say that many of us are not in Christian environments designed to guide us into Stages 4 (including the Wall), 5, and 6.

It appears that, in fact, we are suffering from a "Great Omission."

If we are called to become disciples and make more, we cannot simply stop with diagnosing the problem. How does a person move from choosing to follow Jesus, learning about Him, and doing some service for Him into these later stages, culminating in a life that's extraordinary, powerful, sacrificial, and loving like His?

The World of Ideas

Let's pause here for a confession.

What follows may seem like an unexpected turn into uncharted territory. We could easily begin exploring Bible studies, sacraments, liturgy, Scripture memorization, and all the other things Christians are rightfully taught to do to become mature disciples. Those are all very worth exploring, and there are untold numbers of books, videos, resources, and courses designed to help us with them.

At the same time, if we are facing a startling shortage of people becoming more like Jesus, perhaps we should engage some paths on this journey that aren't as well trodden.

So, we're going to dig into a world that has received shockingly little attention in modern Christianity (and society in general). It's a world that defines and governs us, that dictates how we view reality, life, and other people. And it's a world that not only powers individuals but also entire nations and cultures.

It's the world of *Ideas*.

I mentioned in the introduction that, as our family was amid our dark night and I was floundering against the Wall, I came across a book by Dallas Willard called *Renovation of the Heart*. Willard delivers a fascinating look at what drives our spiritual formation, and it doesn't sound like most of what we hear about in modern Christianity. He teaches that, at the very root of our spiritual formation, we don't find doctrine, theology, or even belief. We find Ideas.

He doesn't mean "Ideas" like our "aha" moments when we suddenly form a new thought or solution. He isn't referring to the metaphorical lightbulb over our heads. He means assumptions and principles buried deep in the recesses of our hearts. Hidden, somewhat mysterious things. Things of which we aren't even normally conscious.

That got my attention. And I didn't particularly like the thought that I was powered and governed by concepts of which I wasn't even aware.

Then, I discovered Willard wasn't the first person to explore Ideas.

In fact, Ideas have been the subject of discussion and debate dating back to early philosophers and theologians, people like Plato, Aristotle, Descartes, Augustine, Aquinas, Kierkegaard, and Calvin.

Ideas are at work in individual hearts, families, communities, cultures, and nations. And most of us don't know they're there.

For our purposes, let's adopt this definition:

An Idea is a fundamental concept, assumption, or principle in which our hearts are rooted but of which we are generally unaware.

It is also essential to understand that Ideas are *not so much intellectual conclusions as they are experienced and relational realities.*

Ideas are critical and foundational to our human experience, and uncovering our hidden Ideas is a crucial step on our journey to becoming more like Jesus.

Willard wrote, "Ideas are so essential to how we approach life that we often do not understand when and how Ideas are at work... [People] don't know what moves them, but Ideas govern them and have their consequences anyway."[5]

Our hearts embrace Ideas about freedom, about science, about God. We have Ideas about love, sex, culture, and marriage. We have Ideas about what it means to be human.

If you were born in the West, you were born into the Idea that women may vote. We assume it. We rarely think about it. We operate our lives accepting this Idea as an experienced reality. But for much of human history, people were born into an atmosphere with an entirely different Idea. It would have been foolish or unthinkable that a woman would have any role in government or public affairs in many cultures.

You were also born into the Idea that, on the whole, children are good for the world and society. We take great care to feed and nurture our children, to educate them. We don't think about it. It is our experienced, accepted reality.

But, again, many ancient cultures viewed children (particularly girls) as a burden or as a means to an end, whether it be the propagation of our species, labor, or even sexual gratification. Their "Idea" of children was very different from ours. It would have been laughable to educate a child or to honor a child. They didn't think about it. It was just the way things were.

Another example is the traffic light, which represents various Ideas. We assume and expect people to pay attention to the colors on the light and operate their cars accordingly. It's an Idea we're all born into. It's our experienced reality. But if you drive your car in some countries in the world, there either are no traffic lights, or they're considered optional!

Or consider our modern culture's accepted assumptions about science and rationality. If something can't be proven, it has less value. If something can't be rationalized, it is rejected (though this Idea has arguably been changing in recent years).

This type of unconscious assumption about reality differs greatly from how other epochs (primarily the Middle Ages) understood reality, where the supernatural was as "real" as the natural. Where "values" were more rock solid than "facts."

We operate in a world of unconscious Ideas. They form our experienced and relational reality. There are dozens upon dozens of categories of Ideas: time, origin, government, value, roles, behavior, power, identity, anthropology, purpose, authority, law, love, justice, and so on.

These Ideas have a foundational impact on our relationship with God, with ourselves, with others, and even with creation. Ideas are profoundly embedded in our relationship with Christianity.

Ideas and the Bible

We also have ingrained Ideas about our church experience and our theology. Some of these Ideas are found in the Bible, while others are traditional or even cultural.

Here are a few examples.

Have you ever been told that the apostle Paul wrote the majority of the New Testament? Somewhere around 75 percent? Is that a correct Idea? In terms of the number of books, Paul did write the majority of them. But what about the number of *words*? What about the actual percentage of content in the New Testament?

In that case, Paul is not the author of the majority of the New Testament. Luke is. The accuracy of this Idea boils down to our assumed definition of the word "majority." If you assume the word "majority" indicates "number of books" in this context, Paul is the correct answer. But if you assume the word "majority" here means "overall content," and you believe the majority writer was Paul, your "Idea" (assumed conclusion) about who wrote most of the New Testament is incorrect.

That Idea may or may not impact how you relate to the New Testament, but here's an example of an Idea that significantly influences how we engage the Bible.

Years ago, I was chatting with a biblically literate friend, and he expressed frustration that people are still writing all sorts of books *about* the Bible. His view is that we now know all we need to know about Scripture and that we simply need to spend more time in the Word itself. We should stop writing books about it.

You may have heard a pastor mention this type of conclusion in a sermon or two, normally with some frustration: we need to read fewer books *about* the Bible and spend more time *in the actual* Bible. In other words, we should spend more time in the Word itself rather than in extra-biblical explanations of the text.

This is ironic, considering every sermon is, by definition, an extra-biblical explanation of a biblical text. And if we've discovered even five or ten percent of the Bible's vast riches of depth, wisdom, and mystery, I'd be surprised.

We *should* spend more time in the Word. However, do we unconsciously approach the Bible with the *Idea* that it has already been fully explored? Or do we approach it with the Idea that its depths have yet to be mined? The answer makes a profound difference in how we relate to the Word.

Should we stop exploring and probing the depths of God's "second book" of creation?[6] Previous generations of Christians spent far more time in and around nature, identifying and celebrating God's characteristics that He wove into the created order.

American theologian and thinker Jonathan Edwards wrote:

> Now we have shown that the Son of God created the world for this very end, to communicate Himself in an image of His own excellency. The beauties of nature are really emanations, or shadows, of the excellencies of the Son of God.
>
> So that when we are delighted with flowery meadows and gentle breezes of wind, we may consider that we only see the emanations of the sweet benevolence of Jesus Christ. When we behold the fragrant rose and lily, we see His love and purity.
>
> So the green trees and fields, and singing of birds, are the emanations of His infinite joy and benignity. The easiness and naturalness of trees and vines are shadows of His infinite beauty and loveliness. The crystal rivers and murmuring streams have the footsteps of His sweet grace and bounty.[7]

Have we learned all we need to know about the created order? Have we learned all there is to know about biology or sociology, the human brain, the far reaches of space, or even the depths of the ocean? (According to oceanographers, less than 20 percent of the Earth's oceans have been researched so far.)

When we approach the Bible, do we approach it with the *Idea* that everything that should be known about it is already known? Or dare we plumb its depths, assuming that its mysteries, its applications, and its power to move us are still as unexplored as the oceans?

We approach sacred Scripture with all sorts of unconscious assumptions, including Ideas related to its core purpose. Before reading on, take a moment to ask yourself this question: what do I assume is the primary function of the Bible?

If you've ever been trained to preach a sermon or lead a Bible study, chances are you've been instructed to present three instructional components to your audience: observation, interpretation, and application.

- What does the text say?
- What does the text mean?
- What is the text telling me to do?

This is, by far, the predominant and accepted approach to teaching the Bible today: observe, interpret, apply.

Chances are the overwhelming number of sermons and teachings you, your parents, and your grandparents heard were based on this simple formula. In fact, if we aren't taught some sort of application at the end of a sermon, we may feel like we've been cheated. Someone needs to tell us *what to do*.

Fair enough. But if most sermons are based on this formula, and that formula must include a charge to go and do something because of what we've just heard or read, what do our hearts *assume* about the purpose of the Bible? What is our unconscious *Idea* about the primary function of God's Word?

The answer is *an instruction manual*. The Bible becomes a book of commands. Every verse, every passage, and every chapter must contain something that I must *apply* in my life. Cause and effect: the Bible says "x," so I need to go and do "y." This becomes our unconscious Idea, our accepted view of reality.

In fact, some of us have been taught that B.I.B.L.E. stands for "Basic Instructions Before Leaving Earth."

But if this view of the Word is true, then why is 40-some percent of the Bible written as a narrative, as a story? Why is 30-some percent of the Bible poetry? When was the last time we read Dickinson or Whitman or Keats and walked away thinking, "Here are the three things I learned from this poem that I need to *do* this week"?

Does the Bible contain instructions for living? Of course. There are numerous verses with guidance on how to live our lives. But is that its sole or even primary purpose?

The Power of Ideas

Just how powerful are these Ideas? How much do they influence us, our behaviors, our words, and what or whom we love?

Willard, in citing Ephesians 6:12, writes:

> The apostle Paul warned that "our struggle is not against flesh and blood, but against the rulers, against the powers, against the world forces of this darkness, against the spiritual forces of wickedness in the heavenly places." These powers and forces are spiritual agencies that work with the *idea systems of evil. These systems are the powers' main tool for dominating humanity.*[8]

Nineteenth-century French poet and author Victor Hugo wrote, "An invasion of armies can be resisted, but not an invasion of ideas."[9] Or, as noted American civil rights activist Medgar Evers puts it, "You can kill a man, but you can't kill an idea."[10]

If Ideas are this powerful, this foundational to our hearts and how we embrace the world, it's imperative we explore their role in our spiritual formation. As apprentices of Jesus for the purpose of becoming more like Him, what role do Ideas play in our spiritual journey?

Willard wrote, "The process of spiritual formation in Christ is one of *progressively* replacing those destructive images and ideas with the images and ideas that filled the mind of Jesus Himself."[11]

Discipleship is a process of replacing bad Ideas with good ones, replacing dark Ideas with light ones.

Though as powerful as Ideas are, transforming them is far from easy.

> Changing those governing ideas is one of the most difficult and painful things in life... Jesus confronted and undermined an idea system and its culture, which in turn killed him. He proved himself greater than any idea system or culture, and he lives on. He is continuing the process of a worldwide idea shift that is crucial to *his* perpetual revolution, in which we each are assigned a part.[12]

Indeed, Jesus taught, modeled, and confronted a dizzying array of Ideas when He came to rescue and redeem the earth. He confronted Ideas about the value of women and children and the role of human beings in creation. He upended Ideas about politics and protocols, power, and popularity. He tackled Ideas about justice, poverty, shame, identity, leadership, love, time, priorities, service, sacrifice, wrath, peace, redemption, reconciliation, history, and the future.

He talked in parables and paradoxes, constantly provoking and challenging the unconscious assumptions of both governing structures and individual hearts.

Once we start wrapping our minds and hearts around the existence of unconscious Ideas and the power they hold in individuals, families, cultures, and nations, we begin to identify them everywhere. And we read the Bible with new eyes. And we soon discover just how vital the uncovering of Ideas in our hearts is in our discipleship journey.

Let's return to our three key questions about discipleship.

What is a disciple? An apprentice of Jesus.

Why should we be a disciple and make others? So that we and others can become more like Jesus through spiritual formation.

And how are disciples made? How do we experience the later stages of our formation, resulting in living our lives as if Jesus was living them? We do so through *the progressive transformation of the unconscious, highly influential Ideas that sit in the bedrock of our hearts.*

The Deep Disciple

It may take a while to embrace the world of Ideas. Many, if not most, people don't become conscious of Ideas, whether in their culture or in their hearts. We simply plow through life, attempting to navigate our day-to-day work and interactions without pausing to dig deeper into these unconscious assumptions that govern us and our societies.

Yet, if Willard is correct, Jesus came and confronted a distorted Idea system and knew precisely what He was doing. Not only did He fully comprehend the Ideas that were at work in the Jewish nation as they struggled under Roman occupation (as well as those of Rome itself), but He also had an uncanny ability to quickly discern the Ideas in the hearts of those around Him.

And we, as His apprentices, are to join with Him in continuing His work of identifying both cultural and individual Ideas, transforming bad ones (those that do not align with Christ's example, character, purpose, and will) into good ones (those that do).

This is most likely not the concept of discipleship to which we're accustomed.

However, it may be the key to unlocking the "more" of the Christian life for which many of us are longing. Perhaps the path through the Wall into the deeper stages of our journey with Jesus is one in which we search the heart of Jesus, others, culture, and ourselves to uncover these hidden Ideas and, somehow, progressively transform the harmful ones into Ideas that bring flourishing and goodness.

Throughout the book, you'll notice a few terms and usage that may not be familiar. There is a "Terms and Definitions" section at the back if you need a quick reference guide.

We've already begun to explore the concept of "Ideas" and how they relate to our spiritual journey. Here's the next new term: "Deep Discipleship."

The word "discipleship" is so overloaded with definitions, overtones, and historical meaning that it often loses its primacy in the confusion. Many people unconsciously assume that if we're "converted," we're automatically disciples, or they use the words as synonyms. In other words, in this assumption, if you're a believer in Christ as the Son of God, you're a disciple.

To cut through some of the overuse and confusion, we'll define Deep Discipleship as the journey of someone whose life is consumed with becoming more like Jesus. Someone whose life is centered around seeking Jesus and His kingdom. Someone who explores the Ideas and desires in their hearts and passionately seeks to see them transformed into the Ideas and desires of Jesus. Someone who wants to learn to do the things Jesus did.

This doesn't describe the so-called "consumer Christian"—the person who goes to church on Sunday and then goes about her life, segmenting the rest of her existence from her church experience.

This doesn't describe the "carnal Christian"—the person who claims to follow Jesus, yet willfully remains in behaviors, habits, and relationships that contradict the goodness He has for us.

This doesn't even necessarily describe the doctrinally sound Christian. Many people strive for theological accuracy, yet don't strive to assume the character of Jesus, to become more like Him.

The "Deep Disciple" may not be the person who shows up at church the most, volunteers the most, or has memorized the most Scripture.

In some ways, a person engaged in Deep Discipleship may be someone who finds themselves in Stages 4, 5, or 6 in their critical journey. Most likely, a Deep Disciple has experienced at least one "Wall" and has entered the suffering and introspection the Wall offers.

"Deep Discipleship" is not a statement of value. Someone embracing Deep Discipleship is not worth more than someone in earlier stages or someone who is struggling with consumer or carnal Christianity.

Someone engaged in Deep Discipleship is in the process of surrendering their lives, is willing to engage their own story and history as part of their journey, is open to exploring the Ideas in their hearts, others' hearts, and church and culture, and is comfortable embracing doubts, disagreements, and suffering. Most likely, they have already suffered.

A person engaging in Deep Discipleship has a thirst to know others' stories. They have a thirst for exploring God as He has revealed Himself in both the Bible and His second book of creation.

A friend of mine considers someone like this to be "awake." They are awake to the heart of God, to their own hearts, and to the hearts of others. At Soil & Roots, we often say this person desires to "dig beneath the surface." They are aware of Ideas and desires beneath the ground of our polished exteriors, and they're courageously curious to uncover deeper things, both in people and in cultures.

Next, we'll dissect this concept of Ideas, so that we may better understand how they are progressively transformed.

Chapter 2 Cumulative Key Takeaways

1. We often experience a disconnection from God, others, ourselves, and creation. We wonder if there's something more to the Christian life.

2. A primary reason for this struggle is because the West suffers from the "Great Omission," a struggle to genuinely make people who live and love like Jesus.
3. A disciple is an apprentice of Jesus for the purpose of becoming more like Him. This journey is called "spiritual formation" or "character formation."
4. This spiritual journey may be described in six stages. Yet church institutions almost exclusively focus on Stages 1–3. This leaves Christians unprepared and confused when we inevitably encounter a crisis, or "the Wall."
5. One way to describe the journey of Stages 4–6 is called Deep Discipleship. It involves exploring, uncovering, and transforming powerful assumptions and principles called Ideas.

---

1. Ashley Abercrombie, "Finding God In The Hard Places," *YouVersion*, accessed October 19, 2023, https://www.bible.com/reading-plans/3137-finding-god-in-the-hard-places/day/1.
2. Hagberg, J., & Guelich, R. (2005). *The Critical Journey: Stages in the Life of Faith* (p. 93). Sheffield Publishing Company.
3. Hagberg, J., & Guelich, R. (2005). *The Critical Journey* (pp. 114—115). Sheffield Publishing Company.
4. Hagberg, J., & Guelich, R. (2005). *The Critical Journey* (pp. 152—153). Sheffield Publishing Company.
5. Willard, D. (2012). *Renovation of the Heart* (p. 97). NavPress.
6. Theologians call nature God's "second book," and it's also referred to as God's "general revelation."
7. Jonathan Edwards, "The Excellency of Christ," Tollelege.net, accessed November 7, 2023, https://tollelege.net/2013/08/07/the-excellency-of-christ-in-the-beauties-of-nature-by-jonathan-edwards/.
8. Willard. *Renovation of the Heart* (p. 98). (emphasis mine)
9. Hugo, V. *History of a Crime.*
10. Mrs. Medgar W. Evers, *National Association for the Advancement of Colored People*, accessed October 20, 2023, https://www.crmvet.org/docs/63_naacp_killaman.pdf.
11. Willard, D., & Johnson, J. (2006). *Renovation of the Heart in Daily Practice: Experiments in Spiritual Transformation* (p. 72). NavPress.
12. Willard, D., & Johnson, J. (2006). *Renovation of the Heart in Daily Practice: Experiments in Spiritual Transformation* (pp. 68–69). NavPress.

Three
The Anatomy Of Ideas

Ideas are the greatest and most crucially practical power on earth.

—Ayn Rand[1]

By now, you may have uncovered the purpose behind the name of the book and the organization, "Soil & Roots."

Our hearts, our spirits, are at the core of who we are, the central human element from which we operate and orient ourselves in reality. Springs of life flow from them. So, we might say our hearts are our roots. Like roots, our hearts are deep beneath our surface, hidden from view, and seek nourishment, connectedness, and life from the soil.

What is the soil? The Ideas and desires that power and govern us.

Soil and roots. The Ideas that animate us and their interaction with the core of our humanity, our hearts.

We've discovered, however, that we're largely unaware of these Ideas that power and govern us. We might find that disconcerting, so let's dig further into the anatomy of Ideas to understand what they are and how they influence us.

We'll consider four pivotal questions about Ideas:

1. Origin – Where do Ideas come from?
2. Location – Where can we find these Ideas?
3. Formation – How do our hearts embrace various Ideas?
4. Awareness – How may we identify the Ideas in our soil?

Origin of Ideas

Soil & Roots provides various visual resources to help our communities, readers, and listeners engage with our discussions on spiritual formation.

Let's take a look at an important image we call the "Creation Picture." (You may also find it at www.soilandroots.org.)

This simple nature drawing illustrates how we live and grow in the reality in which God has placed us.

- The outside circle represents all of creation and the cosmos.
- The seven mountains in the background represent culture, which can be divided into seven primary areas: family,

church, business, media, government, arts & entertainment, and education.

- The tree in the foreground represents you.
- The other trees represent other people in your life. This includes your close family, friends, co-workers, and others you may develop relationships with over time.
- This picture is a "cutaway" drawing, in that you can see things beneath the surface we otherwise wouldn't see. Below the ground, you'll see the roots of your tree. These roots represent your heart.
- Your roots are planted in the soil. The soil represents the countless Ideas that surround and are embraced by your heart.

The picture also helps us understand the four relationships in which God has placed us. We have a relationship with Him (the invisible author of the picture), other people, ourselves, and creation.

So, where do Ideas come from, and how do they fit into our picture?

The Two Kingdoms

In Paul's letter to the Colossians, he employs wonderfully regal and majestic language as he paints a picture of Jesus as the rightful King of the Cosmos.

> For He rescued us from the domain of darkness, and transferred us to the kingdom of His beloved Son, in whom we have redemption, the forgiveness of sins. He is the image of the invisible God, the firstborn of all creation. For by Him all things were created, both in the heavens and on earth, visible and invisible, whether thrones or dominions or rulers or authorities —all things have been created through Him and for Him. He is

> before all things, and in Him all things hold together. He is also head of the body, the church; and He is the beginning, the firstborn from the dead, so that He Himself will come to have first place in everything. For it was the Father's good pleasure for all the fullness to dwell in Him, and through Him to reconcile all things to Himself, having made peace through the blood of His cross; through Him, I say, whether things on earth or things in heaven.[2]

Ideas come from one of two places: the kingdom of light and the kingdom (or domain) of darkness. Every Idea, whether we're conscious of it or not, comes from one of these two kingdoms.

Ideas from the kingdom of light are truthful, beautiful, and good. They result in human flourishing.

Ideas from the kingdom of darkness are distortions, corruptions, or abuses of Ideas from the kingdom of light. Ideas of darkness are designed to harm and kill us.

God is the origin of the Ideas of the kingdom of light. In some mysterious way, He *is* Ideas of light. Remember, Ideas are not as much intellectual conclusions as they are experienced or relational realities.

Though there are dozens of categories of Ideas, certain categories tend to define us and how we operate in the world. We call these the "Six Core Ideas." They are:

- Identity: Who are we?
- Anthropology: What are we?
- Value: What are we worth?
- Power: What authority do we have?
- Purpose: Why are we?
- Love: What and whom do we love?

These Six Core Ideas form the basis of every "Idea system." An Idea system is a collection of individual Ideas, typically codified into a cohesive understanding of reality. Buddhism, Marxism, Socialism, Capitalism, and most other "isms" are Idea systems. Christianity is also an Idea system.

When our hearts embrace Ideas of light in these six core categories, we experience freedom and joy. Our desires bend toward God, and we become more like Christ. Our relationship with God deepens, though we also learn to love ourselves, love others well, and have a kingdom impact on creation and culture.

The kingdom of darkness does not and cannot *originate* Ideas. It can only distort Ideas of light. Ideas of darkness are subtle variations, incomplete versions, or contradictions of Ideas of light.

Given the number of superhero movies, we could be forgiven for assuming evil always shows up as a villain dressed in black. Generally speaking, evil is not so easy to spot. Some of the most wicked people I've ever known are also the nicest. They go to church. They pray for their friends. They are usually admired and respected.

Likewise, Ideas of darkness can be very subtle and, on the surface, appear good and healthy. They often appeal to good desires in our hearts, but do so in a way that we are caught off guard by their true intention, which is to harm and kill us.

We find clear examples of Ideas from both kingdoms in the first few chapters of Scripture.

In Genesis 2, we read:

> The Lord God commanded the man, saying, "From any tree of the garden you may eat freely; but from the tree of the knowledge of good and evil you shall not eat, for in the day that you eat from it you will surely die."[3]

Here, we find God presenting Ideas such as generosity (you may eat from any tree), freedom (you may choose between life and death), and clarity (clear consequences of their choices).

However, in Genesis 3, the serpent approaches Eve and distorts God's instructions and His Ideas:

> And he said to the woman, "Indeed, has God said, 'You shall not eat from any tree of the garden'?"
>
> The woman said to the serpent, "From the fruit of the trees of the garden we may eat; but from the fruit of the tree which is in the middle of the garden, God has said, 'You shall not eat from it or touch it, or you will die.'"
>
> The serpent said to the woman, "You surely will not die! For God knows that in the day you eat from it your eyes will be opened, and you will be like God, knowing good and evil."
>
> When the woman saw that the tree was good for food, and that it was a delight to the eyes, and that the tree was desirable to make one wise, she took from its fruit and ate; and she gave also to her husband with her, and he ate.[4]

Let's look at this creation/fall story through the lens of two Ideas: identity and power.

Light Idea of Identity: Adam and Eve are created by God, and they are good. They are made in God's image. They are not divine, though they enjoy an in-person relationship with their Creator. God is their loving Creator, and they are His children.

Light Idea of Power: God gives them stewardship over the earth in Genesis 1. God grants them authority to rule all of creation on His behalf. He does not give them divine authority, however. Adam and Eve are human, not gods. They do not have power over death. They are not omniscient. They cannot define good and evil. They are co-regents with God in the act of refining and managing the earth. The serpent then distorts God's Ideas, twisting them in order to harm Adam and Eve.

Dark Idea of Identity: You can be like God. You can become gods.

Dark Idea of Power: You will not die. You can have power over death.

Instead of presenting God as their loving Creator, the serpent suggests God is a deceitful, power-hungry deity who is keeping Adam and Eve in the dark to protect Himself.

The serpent didn't argue against the existence of God. He didn't present radical *new* Ideas. He presented subtle variations of God's Ideas that prompted doubt in Eve's heart.

He appealed to her good desires for food, for pleasing things to look at, and for wisdom. But instead of trusting in God to provide those things, Eve trusted the darkness and ate from the tree, as did Adam. They rejected the Idea of being co-regents with God and elected to take sole reign of the earth.

Sin entered the world, and the kingdom of darkness was, in effect, inaugurated. And that kingdom corrupted everything on the planet.

That's the power of Ideas.

Location

In today's cultural climate, we might wonder where Ideas from the kingdom of light can actually be found. Though God's Ideas are original, and the darkness can only distort what belongs to Him, are dark Ideas more prevalent than light?

Hardly! *Ideas of light are everywhere.* Ideas of light are found in at least five locations:

1. God wrote us a personal book, the Bible. In it, He reveals Ideas about Himself and the world He's made. We call it God's "special revelation." In our technological age, His book is available to us anytime, anywhere.

2. God wrote us another book, the Book of Creation. Theologians call nature God's "second book," and it's also referred to as God's "general revelation."

God puts His Ideas into every cell and into every star. His creation is littered with His Ideas. Yet, in modern Christianity, we aren't normally accustomed to looking for Him in His second book.

Creation displays all sorts of God's Ideas, including creativity, design, love, wonder, purpose, and a myriad of mathematical and scientific principles.

Some Christians become nervous and suspicious when we talk about God's second book, but we shouldn't. Jonathan Edwards is credited as having said, "Nature is God's greatest evangelist."[5]

Modern Christians often steer clear of discussing nature because we fear that any mention of the environment will automatically lead us into nature worship or environmental extremism. Due to this concern, we've swung the pendulum too far, especially considering we can't understand the Bible without a grasp of God's second book. The Bible relies heavily on nature metaphors and imagery, including flora, fauna, astronomy, human anatomy, agriculture, and a host of other creation wonders. Garden and nature imagery pervades Scripture from its beginning to its end.

3. God frequently reveals and shares His good Ideas through other people. He may share His Ideas through our spouses, children, family, close friends, mentors, pastors, other mature leaders, and sometimes complete strangers. God weaves His Ideas into our lives through other people.

C. S. Lewis wrote:

> He works on all of us in all sorts of ways, not only through what we think our "religious life." He works through Nature, through

> our own bodies, through books, sometimes through experiences which seem (at the time) anti-Christian. When a young man who has been going to church in a routine way honestly realizes that he does not believe in Christianity and stops going—provided he does it for honesty's sake and not just to annoy his parents—the spirit of Christ is probably nearer to him then than it ever was before. *But above all, He works on us through each other.*[6]

---

4. Ourselves. We come "pre-loaded" with certain Ideas about life and reality. We may learn some of God's Ideas simply by studying and understanding how we're wired. Think back on neuroscientist Curt Thompson's assertion that we come into the world looking for someone looking for us.

5. Last but certainly not least, God shares His Ideas through Himself. When we follow Jesus, God sends His Spirit to take up residence in ours, and the Spirit teaches, counsels, comforts, and affirms God's Ideas.

We begin to get the sense of just how passionately and purposefully God pursues us. His good, truthful, life-giving Ideas are literally everywhere, both outside and inside us, both in the physical and spiritual realms.

Because Ideas of darkness are not original and are corruptions of Ideas of light, we find dark Ideas in similar places. Both of God's books are often corrupted and misused, leading to dark Ideas. And every person has a mixture of dark and light Ideas in their hearts. So, at any given time, we may be influencing others and ourselves through the spreading of dark Ideas.

We find this conflict articulated in James as he discusses the irony of our tongues, our words.

> For every species of beasts and birds, of reptiles and creatures of the sea, is tamed and has been tamed by the human race. But no one can tame the tongue; it is a restless evil and full of deadly poison. With it we bless our Lord and Father, and with it we curse men, who have been made in the likeness of God; from the same mouth come both blessing and cursing. My brethren, these things ought not to be this way. Does a fountain send out from the same opening both fresh and bitter water? Can a fig tree, my brethren, produce olives, or a vine produce figs? Nor can saltwater produce fresh.[7]

Ideas in the Air and Soil

It's helpful to explore the location of Ideas in another manner. For this, we'll return to our Creation Picture, though we've updated it to include a look at how Ideas flow. This is also available on the Soil & Roots website.

Let's introduce two new terms: Ideas in the Air and Ideas in the Soil.

Ideas in the Air are those generated by creation and culture. **Ideas in the Soil** are those that seep into and form our hearts.

Ideas in the Air are those we're born into. These are greatly impacted by the era, location, and culture into which we arrive. They're also heavily influenced by our family of origin.

An example of an Idea in the Air is the governmental system you're born into. Someone born into communism "breathes" very different Ideas about the role of the individual and the state than does someone born into a democratic system.

At home, someone born into a family of eight children will absorb different Ideas of role, attention, and time than an only child.

In some sense, Ideas in the Soil are a subset of those in the Air, as our hearts come to embrace and absorb them.

Ideas from both the kingdom of light and darkness are found in the air and in our soil.

So, to further expound on Dallas Willard's definition of discipleship, spiritual formation is *the progressive transformation of Ideas in our Soil to align with those of Jesus.*

Formation

We now come to the third aspect of our exploration of the anatomy of Ideas, formation. How do Ideas work their way from the soil into our roots? How are our hearts formed by and through Ideas?

There are three types of Idea formation: **initial**, **abrupt**, and **progressive**.

Initial Formation

As we just noted, we come wired with some Ideas of light.

Scripture tells us, for example, that God has set eternity in the hearts of men. Human beings know we are eternal creatures (though we can and sometimes do suppress this Idea). We are born with Ideas in our hearts regarding our "persistence" (meaning we exist past death).

In Romans 2, Paul shares how even human beings who know nothing of God still have a conscience. We come pre-wired with Ideas about morality, justice, and fairness.

We also come wired with some Ideas of darkness.

If you aren't sure about that, you probably haven't raised a toddler. We don't train our children to lie and steal, but they lie and steal anyhow. We lie and steal when our hearts embrace the wrong Ideas of power and value. Most parents don't teach their two-year-old bad Ideas of power and value; we come with them already in our hearts.

Abrupt Formation

The Ideas in our hearts sometimes change very quickly and dramatically, primarily because of two causes: divine intervention and trauma. Divine intervention results in our hearts embracing Ideas of light. Trauma often (but not always) results in our hearts bending toward Ideas of darkness.

Salvation is a prime example of a divine intervention that results in radical, abrupt changes in our core Ideas. Salvation doesn't always occur quickly, of course, but many times it does. Through this intervention, our core Ideas of identity, anthropology, value, power, purpose, and love all change from darkness to light in various ways and to varying degrees.

When Christ saves us, Ideas of identity in our hearts are changed. We are no longer orphans; we are sons and daughters of God. We give up the notion that we can be gods ourselves and surrender to the Idea that only God is God. Our Ideas of power change: we accept we do not have the power to save ourselves. Only Christ has that power. Our Ideas of purpose change. We may give up our self-centered pursuits in favor of surrendering to whatever purpose God gives us.

On the other hand, trauma can quickly distort and corrupt our hearts and turn them toward darkness. Tragically, our culture continues to see an acceleration of abuse, exploitation, and betrayal, which results in all manner of destruction: self-harm, substance abuse, relationship collapse, suicide, and other forms of violence. These are evidence of profound negative changes in our Core Ideas.

A young girl who is molested will experience seriously harmful, sudden changes to her Ideas of identity, power, and value, at the very least. Her concept of self may be distorted. Her heart may become confused about her powerlessness, and she may struggle with who she is and how her value is determined.

A son whose father abandons the family may experience terrible changes to his Ideas of identity, value, and love. When a father leaves his family, he corrupts a fundamental Idea of what love is: sacrificially giving ourselves to someone else.

The loss of a loved one can cause abrupt changes to our Ideas, as can other losses, such as a failed friendship, job loss, infertility, or illness.

In the case of being victimized, the closer the relationship to the one causing the harm, the deeper and more insidious the changes to the Ideas in our soil. A single instance of harm can certainly cause traumatic changes to our hearts, but prolonged harm may cut even deeper.

If we have ever experienced trauma (whether "big T" or "little t"), we have come to appreciate why time is such an essential component of discipleship.[8] Some Ideas of darkness are so deeply embedded in our hearts because of trauma that it takes long periods of time, the introduction of various life-giving habits, and intimacy with healthy people in a committed community to slowly turn Ideas of darkness into Ideas of light. For some, it's a lifelong process.

We may be harmed through abrupt formation, but we normally don't heal that way. Though God may, at times, choose to heal our hearts quickly, our healing journey is usually progressive.

Progressive Formation

"Progressive Formation" refers to the steady drip of Ideas over long periods of time. In a positive sense, this process happens through the five ways God shares His Ideas: creation, culture, others, Himself, and His Word.

Many Christians who are aware of the progressive formation of Ideas tend to see it in the context of culture's propagation of harmful, dark Ideas.

For example, we may look back at the cultural mountains of media, education, and arts and entertainment to see how various Ideas of darkness have slowly, consistently, relentlessly made their way into our homes and hearts over the past several decades. They have seeped into our soils.

The kingdom of darkness understands the power of Ideas very well and uses various cultural institutions to progressively promote its Ideas with great effectiveness.

Why? Because it's efficient. Using culture to saturate hearts with Ideas of darkness is essentially crop-dusting. Evil may impact millions of hearts at one time by efficiently spreading its Ideas through various mountains and institutions of culture.

Ideas of darkness may also progressively invade our hearts through unhealthy relationships. Women who escape from abusive, long-term situations share how their core Ideas of identity, value, power, purpose, and love were corrupted and damaged by their abuser and how it may take years of healthy, life-giving engagement to embrace core Ideas of light.

Ideas of light progressively influence our hearts as well, and this is beautiful to experience. If you've ever had the privilege of walking with a friend or family member through a crisis or relationship that harmed their hearts, chances are you have watched God gently invite the victim back to Ideas of light through your relationship, other caring friends, Scripture, life circumstances, prayer, and your simple presence amid the victim's pain.

Awareness

Lastly, how do we become aware of the hidden Ideas in our hearts?

Generally, most of us don't come to realize hidden Ideas govern our hearts until we're faced with a crisis that calls our conscious assumptions into question. We hit the Wall.

Even faced with a crisis, many of us still don't explore the hidden Ideas that are being tested and challenged. Instead, we develop and implement various coping mechanisms to avoid doing the hard work of identifying and experiencing the hidden Ideas that drive us.

When faced with grief, illness, job loss, divorce, abuse, financial stress, betrayal, abandonment, war, or some other crisis of life and faith, we will often push down the doubts, dissensions, and deep questions that inevitably arise. Instead, we engage in various activities and habits to "push past" the confusion and disorientation lying just beneath the surface. The process of exploring our Ideas may be painful, and we don't wish to be in pain.

We often accomplish this distraction or "pushing past" by increasing our amount of activity. This may take the form of work, hobbies, travel, or new projects. For the Christian, this often looks like a deeper commitment to service. The modern church frequently de-emphasizes exploring our own stories and journeys in favor of serving others. The underlying conclusion is that "the best way to move past a crisis is to pour yourself into other people."

Though often a recipe for further breakdown and harm, that approach remains a spoken or unspoken mantra of modern Christianity. Imagine asking a surgeon with a broken arm to perform surgery on someone else suffering from a broken arm. It would make far more sense for the surgeon to heal first before healing others.

Other coping mechanisms may come into play, including pornography and alcohol and drug addiction. As one mental health professional told me years ago, "I've never seen an opioid addict who wasn't suffering from some sort of trauma. Addiction is always a response to inner harm and wounds that go unexplored and unhealed."

In our age of prosperity, leisure, information, and entertainment, our options for applying coping mechanisms are nearly endless. Most people, Christian or otherwise, are reluctant to do the deep heart exploration necessary for genuine freedom, opting rather to deflect and depress their hidden Ideas in favor of creative coping mechanisms.

Ideas and Beliefs

An example from my own story reveals the way a crisis revealed how a hidden Idea in my heart differed radically from my intellectual belief.

I've served organizations in leadership roles over the years, and at one point, I was running one that faced some painful challenges. On top of that, I was dealing with a personal situation involving a close friend and felt like I had to make some no-win decisions. I couldn't find a way to resolve a difficult set of circumstances without someone being hurt and our friendship falling apart. Other relationships were also at risk.

This had been going on for several weeks, and I was starting to fray. I had been shouldering these challenges well on the outside, but inside, I was falling apart.

Our water bill is perpetually high, and I'm the reason. I think, debate, and process life in the shower. One morning before work, I was showering and attempting to determine what to do with all these seemingly impossible circumstances. Suddenly, the weight of my role, the decisions I had to make, the emotional strain, and the hurt that was sure to come all crashed into my soul. Though I'm typically a composed person, I collapsed onto the shower floor and began to weep uncontrollably.

My wife Jessica woke up in the next room when she heard me gasping. She rushed into the bathroom, saw me on the floor of the shower, and without a second thought she opened the door, sat down, and grabbed me as hard as she could. And she just held me. She didn't say a word; she just sat there, fully clothed in her pajamas, soaking wet, holding me.

I have attended a few thousand worship services in my life. I have been in prayer service after prayer service. As a church musician, I have also participated in numerous types of worship experiences, ranging from pipe organs and hymns to worship bands and dancing.

In all my years, I have never had a more worshipful experience than I did that morning. I have never experienced a more powerful expression of Jesus's love for me than my wife rushing to meet me in my grief and anxiety, taking me as I was, getting herself and her clothes soaking wet, and just holding me. Just being with me.

That crisis became a milestone in the transformation of an Idea of darkness in my heart.

If you had asked me five or six years prior to that morning if God loved me, I would have said absolutely yes. I've known that since I was six. If you had asked me if I had to do anything to earn God's favor, I would have said no. I could not and did not earn God's favor. Jesus earned that on my behalf.

If you had told me that I was, in the hidden recess of my heart, embracing an Idea of love that was more dark than light, I would have vigorously denied it.

But I was. Even though I intellectually knew God loved me, and there was nothing I could do to earn His favor, even though I had been taught that dozens and dozens of times, my heart was holding on to a different Idea. My heart unconsciously embraced the Idea that God loved me *if I performed for Him*, that His acceptance of me was based on what I did for Him. My heart and my head were in two very different places, and I didn't even know it. My conscious belief was very different from my unconscious Idea.

That morning, when my wife rushed in to be with me, was a pivotal moment in my heart's journey. Jessica didn't care if I performed for her. Her love for me wasn't dependent on my good decisions or my poor ones. It didn't matter if I succeeded or failed; it didn't matter if I had lots of friends or had none. She loves me because she loves me. I didn't just *know* it. I *experienced* it.

In the years since that moment, God has continued to use the catalyst of that crisis to reform my heart. My heart is experiencing progressive formation toward an Idea of light.

To frame discipleship this way, the progressive transformation of dark Ideas into light ones, may be new to you.

However, as A. W. Tozer wrote:

> That our Idea of God corresponds as nearly as possible to the true being of God is of immense importance to us. Compared with our actual thoughts about Him, our creedal statements are of little consequence. Our real Idea of God may lie buried under the rubbish of conventional religious notions and may require an intelligent and vigorous search before it is finally unearthed and exposed for what it is. Only after an ordeal of painful self-probing are we likely to discover what we actually believe about God.[9]

There is often a difference between what we intellectually and emotionally hold to about reality and what our genuine, bedrock Ideas are concerning reality.

Ideas and Story

If we embrace the concept that spiritual formation is primarily about the transformation of Ideas, we might reasonably ask if there are certain periods in our lives when our hearts are more susceptible to Idea formation. There is, in fact, a time in our lives when we are more supple, more vulnerable, and more open to the Six Core Ideas.

Understanding that period leads us to conclude that our stories, our histories, and our personal experiences are far more integral to our spiritual formation than we've ever dreamed. To move forward in our journey to become more like Jesus, we may also need to journey backward.

If you were to ask a parent, educator, or sociologist to identify the most crucial time in a person's formation, they would most likely answer "early childhood." This makes intuitive sense. Just like our physical bodies experience rapid and highly visible changes between our births and, say, nine or ten years old, our hearts experience rapid assumptions of all sorts of Ideas. Our little hearts are new, supple, and ready for intimacy and relationship. And, just like our muscles and bones over time, our hearts begin to solidify and harden as we grow and mature.

Therefore, our families of origin are the primary source of our core Ideas, and early childhood is, in the vast majority of cases, the most formative time of our lives.

For most of us, our hearts assume the Six Core Ideas very early in our existence: identity, anthropology, value, power, purpose, and love.

These Core Ideas don't settle into our hearts just because we've been provided answers and instruction. Our Core Ideas about ourselves, others, God, and creation are molded into our hearts primarily through relationships and experience.

This has far-reaching implications for our journey into Deep Discipleship.

If, for example, your father figure was healthy, loving, attuned, and strongly desired to know you and your heart, you most likely have little challenge experiencing the love of a heavenly Father. You may find experiential intimacy with God to come easily, and your heart is secure in its attachment to Him.

If, however, your father figure was unhealthy, absent, disengaged, or had little desire to pursue you and your heart, you may well have a conscious or unconscious challenge relating to the secure and passionate love from your heavenly Father. You may intellectually agree He pursues you for your good, but that fact is difficult to feel, embrace, or experience. And this lack of relational attachment to God may result in doubts about Him, yourself, or the validity of your faith.

Our stories play an enormous role in forming the Ideas and desires in our hearts and thus play a vital role in our ongoing spiritual formation.

Discipleship is rarely explored or explained in these terms. More often than not, our "Ideas" about discipleship involve "pressing forward," Christian rituals, study, and prayer. While valuable and worthwhile, these practices rarely explore the hidden Ideas in our hearts, how they were formed through our stories, their impact on our four relationships now (God, others, self, creation), and how dark Ideas may be formed into light Ideas as we move ahead.

As a practical exercise, let's take just one deeply held and pervasive Idea and explore it. Let's take a look at the central message of the Christian faith, the Gospel, and determine if our *Idea* of the Gospel is the same thing as the Gospel.

Chapter 3 Cumulative Key Takeaways

1. We often experience a disconnection from God, others, ourselves, and creation. A primary reason for this struggle is that the West suffers from the "Great Omission," a struggle to genuinely make people who live and love like Jesus.
2. Our spiritual formation primarily takes place in the hidden recesses of our hearts, a place that is governed by unconscious Ideas. To explore these Ideas is to engage in Deep Discipleship.
3. There are six core categories of Ideas that tend to govern us: identity, anthropology, value, power, purpose, and love. These six categories are also found in every major Idea system in world history.
4. Ideas come from one of two kingdoms: light or darkness. Ideas in the Air are those found in creation and culture (including our families). Ideas in the Soil are those that

mold and form our hearts. We come "hard-wired" with some Ideas of light and darkness, though abrupt formation (divine intervention and trauma) may occur. Most of the time, Ideas in our hearts are transformed progressively.
5. Ideas for goodness and human flourishing come from the kingdom of light. Ideas from the kingdom of darkness are distortions of Ideas of light, and they are designed to kill us.
6. Most often, the Ideas in our hearts are formed over time. However, many people aren't aware of their hidden Ideas and, even if they are, choose coping mechanisms over the harder journey of exploring their hearts.

---

1. "Ayn Rand Quotes," *AZ Quotes*, accessed October 20, 2023, https://www.azquotes.com/quote/814205.
2. Colossians 1:13–20
3. Genesis 2:16–17
4. Genesis 3:1–6
5. Jason Hardin, "God's Greatest Evangelist," *InGod'sImage*, accessed October 20, 2023, https://www.ingodsimage.com/2008/03/gods-greatest-evangelist/.
6. Lewis, C. S. (1980). *Mere Christianity* (p. 190). HarperOne. (italics mine)
7. James 3:7–12
8. See page 121 for more information.
9. Willard, D. (2002). *Renovation of the Heart: Putting on the Character of Christ* (p. 100). NavPress.

Four
The Idea Of The Gospel

> We have, alas, belittled the cross, imagining it merely as a mechanism for getting us off the hook of our own petty naughtiness or as an example of some general benevolent truth. It is much, much more.
>
> —N. T. Wright[1]

Since these unconscious assumptions, these Ideas, are so essential to human nature and to our spiritual formation, let's examine just one very prominent example in our church and culture today—the Idea of the Gospel.

When I teach Soil & Roots classes, I generally open the first session with these questions:

1. What is the Gospel?
2. What is the kingdom?

It may sound far-fetched, but how we answer these questions

reveals a great deal about how we view Jesus, His purpose, our purpose, and our view of the world and reality. And many Christians' Ideas *about* the Gospel differ from its actual comprehensive nature.

In fact, to answer the first question, it's essential to explore the second.

What is this Kingdom of Light?

We may not hear much about the kingdom of God today, which is ironic. It's a primary theme throughout the Bible.

References to this kingdom appear over 80 times in the New Testament. In fact, regal-sounding words such as "king," "kingdom," "reign," "rule," "authority," "subdue," "crown," "majesty," and "govern" populate much of the entire Bible, from Genesis 1 through Revelation 22.

Jesus instructs us to "seek first the kingdom of God," according to Matthew 6:33.

In response to His disciples' question about how to pray, the very first thing Jesus instructs us to ask for is the coming of His kingdom here to earth, and this kingdom is mentioned again at the end of the prayer (popularly called "The Lord's Prayer" and found in Matthew 6:9-13).

Theologian R. C. Sproul wrote:

> The theme of the kingdom of God is a central motif that runs as a thread through both Old and New Testaments... The Old Testament points to the kingdom as coming in the future. The New Testament opens with the announcement of John the Baptist that "the kingdom of heaven is at hand" (Matthew 3:2)... The New Testament indicates that the kingdom of God is both present and future. There is an "already" and a "not yet" to the kingdom... We serve a King who has already been enthroned. Yet we await His

triumphal return in glory when every knee will bow before Him.[2]

Some Kingdom History

Back in Genesis, God established creation and placed humanity into four relationships with God, the self, others, and creation.

They were all good. Then, the serpent appeared and introduced other Ideas. Mankind sinned, and essentially, the kingdom of darkness was spawned on earth. The curse of this new kingdom impacted more than our relationship with God; it infected all four relationships. The entire cosmos was created good, though the entire cosmos experienced corruption because of sin.

Mankind was separated from God, all four relationships were broken, and evil flourished. Genesis chapters three through eleven detail increasing madness, chaos, murder, and harm.

God raised Israel through Abraham, and God continued to unveil His plan for rescuing and restoring the cosmos. Israel had a tumultuous history, and they ended up repeatedly proving how their kings and nation failed to fulfill God's desires and purpose for them. And then came the intertestamental period, 400 years of silence between the Old and New Testaments.

At a most unexpected time and from a most unexpected place came an unexpected King to implement His kingdom and to restore what was broken in the Garden.

During His three-year ministry, Jesus systematically and lovingly dispelled and destroyed the pervasive Ideas of darkness and introduced (or perhaps re-introduced) the Ideas of His new kingdom.

This was announced as good news—what we call "the Gospel."

And, very often in the Bible, the word "Gospel" is specifically paired with the phrase "of the kingdom."

The Gospel is the good news... of the kingdom. This good news proclaimed that a King had come, and He incepted a new kingdom.

A Reduced Gospel?

This announcement may differ from our assumed *Idea* of "the Gospel," that Jesus came to save us from our sins and is our personal Savior. We may already get the sense that the Gospel of the kingdom is more comprehensive.

Let's look at it from another angle. Though God placed us in four relationships, all four of these relationships were broken in the Garden of Eden.

How many of these four relationships did Jesus come to reconcile in His new kingdom? Did He only come to restore us to God, or did His life, death, resurrection, and ascension have an impact on our other three relationships?

In his letter to the Colossians, Paul addresses the existence of the two kingdoms, Jesus's relation to them both, and what He is up to. Here it is again:

> For He rescued us from the domain of darkness, and transferred us to the kingdom of His beloved Son, in whom we have redemption, the forgiveness of sins. He is the image of the invisible God, the firstborn of all creation. For by Him all things were created, both in the heavens and on earth, visible and invisible, whether thrones or dominions or rulers or authorities —all things have been created through Him and for Him. He is before all things, and in Him all things hold together. He is also head of the body, the church; and He is the beginning, the firstborn from the dead, so that He Himself will come to have first place in everything. For it was the Father's good pleasure for all the fullness to dwell in Him, and through Him to reconcile all things to Himself, having made peace through the blood of His cross; through Him, I say, whether things on earth or things in heaven.[3]

In their book *When Helping Hurts*, Steve Corbett and Brian Fikkert note:

> We have asked thousands of evangelical Christians in numerous contexts this most basic question—why did Jesus come to earth? —and the vast majority of people say something like, "Jesus came to die on the cross to save us from our sins so that we can go to heaven." While this answer is true, Jesus' message is an even more grand and sweeping epic than that...
>
> In this passage [Colossians 1 above], Jesus Christ is described as the Creator, Sustainer, and Reconciler of *everything*. Yes, Jesus died for our souls, but He also died to reconcile—that is, to put into right relationship—all that He created...
>
> The curse is cosmic in scope, bringing decay, brokenness, and death to every speck in the universe. But as King of kings and Lord of lords, Jesus is making all things new! This is the good news of the gospel.[4]

Pastor Dr. Jeremy Treat says, "To be saved into God's kingdom is to embrace God's comprehensive rule over every aspect of life. This is a far cry from merely 'asking Jesus into my heart.' It means a new life, a new identity, and a new kingdom."[5]

So, the kingdom is the reconciliation (or the putting back into right relationship) of everything: man's relationship with God, with ourselves, with others, and with creation and culture.

We *are* reconciled to God through Jesus. However, the Gospel of the Kingdom is the proclamation that the entirety of the cosmos is being restored, not only our personal relationship with God.

Is this our "Idea" of the Gospel?

Theologians call a Gospel orientation that focuses only on the redemption of man's relationship with God the "Reductionist Gospel" or the "Gospel of Salvation." The Reductionist Gospel suggests we embrace Christ as Savior, but we don't really embrace Him as Lord of all—over all our relationships and all of creation and culture.

A Gospel Presentation

Our family recently attended the wedding of a family friend, and the pastor presiding over the service announced himself as an evangelist. He made certain that the bride and groom knew Jesus Christ and reaffirmed their commitment to following Him by having them repeat the "Sinner's Prayer."

And then, he gave a Gospel presentation to the congregation during the service, and it went something like this:

"We are sinners. We cannot save ourselves. Jesus Christ came and took our place so that we could be put back into right relationship with God, and our salvation is a free gift from Him. Because we cannot save ourselves and Christ took our place, we just need to decide to follow Jesus, and then we can spend eternity with God in heaven. Will you decide to accept Jesus as your personal Savior today?"

Have you heard the Gospel presented like that? It's the "reduced" Gospel of Salvation.

In modern Christianity, this is, by far, the "Idea of the Gospel." It's the overriding assumption, the concept of the Gospel that most Christians embrace. And it's true. It's just not complete.

We begin our journey apprenticing with Jesus when we repent of our way of doing things and turn and follow Jesus. It is, in a very real way, a reversal of the Garden of Eden. Instead of picking and eating the fruit, declaring our autonomy from God, and proclaiming our own divinity, Jesus restores us to the way things are intended, that we lay down our claims to divinity and proclaim Him as our divine King.

The good news of His kingdom means that once we declare our allegiance to Him, we join a multi-ethnic, global community led by our

King, constantly involved in the inevitable reconciliation of the cosmos, which encompasses all four relationships.

On the Gospel of the Kingdom, Michael Craven wrote:

> The gospel (or "good news") cannot be fully understood and applied apart from the kingdom of God. Once properly connected to the kingdom, we can then understand and recover the full scope and meaning of the gospel. The fact is, we think we understand the gospel in America—but the evidence overwhelmingly suggests that most of us simply do not understand this most fundamental aspect of the Christian faith.
>
> In a tragic turn of events that began in the nineteenth century with the rise of Revivalism, the gospel of the kingdom has suffered a gradual reduction to merely "the gospel," a term meant to emphasize only the personal plan of salvation.
>
> This reduction stripped the gospel of its cosmic dimensions, which transcend one's personal salvation to include the whole of God's redemptive mission in the world (i.e., the *missio Dei*) in which He is making all things new through Christ.
>
> George Hunsberger makes the point, "This separation has made salvation a private event by dividing 'my personal salvation' from the advent of God's healing reign over all the world." In the wake of this reduction, the proclamation of the church went from "Repent, receive Christ, and enter the kingdom of God" to "Invite Jesus into *your* life." The great fallacy is that we do not invite Jesus into our life—He is inviting us into His: His purpose, His work, and His kingdom!
>
> In essence, the church bears witness to the in-breaking reign of God and serves as the instrument by which God is making "everything sad come untrue."
>
> There is an optimism that should naturally flow from the realization that "our God reigns" (see Isaiah 52:7). Sadly, this optimism is, in my estimation, largely absent from the

> evangelical church in America. Many Christians seem to live and think as if Christ has been overcome by the world rather than vice versa (see John 16:33), or that the gates of Hell do indeed prevail against the church. Perhaps by recovering the biblical mission of the church as participation in God's unrelenting reign, we can, once again, be a people who live as more than those who seem to be barely surviving![6]

Much of Western Christianity is very comfortable with the Gospel of Salvation but seems unaware of or ambivalent about the Gospel of the Kingdom. The Gospel of Salvation has been the predominant "Idea" of Christianity in the West for 100 years or more.

Chuck Colson was a high-ranking government official in the Nixon administration, and he went to prison for his involvement in Watergate. Jesus saved him, and Colson spent the rest of his life as a tour de force for the kingdom, starting Prison Fellowship and another organization now called the Colson Center, which trains a global audience on the Christian worldview. The Colson Center also acknowledges the "Idea" that the Gospel has become reduced, and the organization trains people all over the world on how to recognize and articulate the full, comprehensive Gospel.

They compare the Gospel of Salvation with the Gospel of the Kingdom as a "two-stage Gospel" and a "four-stage Gospel."

The Bible is a grand narrative, and it may be described as a story in four parts: Creation, Fall, Redemption, and Restoration.

The Colson Center maintains that modern Christianity tends to assume a "two-stage Gospel," or Fall and Redemption. Man sinned. Jesus saved us on the cross.

The Colson Center teaches we're missing two critical elements of the Gospel: the bookends of Creation and Restoration. The biblical journey is from Garden to Garden, from Eden to Eden, and the watershed intervention that split time in two and reversed the curse is the life, death, resurrection, and ascension of Jesus, not just his life and death.

If we cut out Creation and Restoration from the narrative of the Gospel, we're missing vital parts of the kingdom story that are necessary for Deep Discipleship. In some sense, the full Gospel involves not just what we're saved from and for whom, but what we're saved into. Our purpose is not only to invite people to apprentice with Jesus; it's also to join with Jesus as He redeems the entire universe.

Impacts of the Reduced Gospel

Ideas have consequences.

Here is just one example of how the "reduced" Idea of the Gospel in our soil impacts the world.

For the last several years, there have been frequent news articles about people leaving churches and how church institutions are concerned about decreasing attendance, particularly of younger people. Various research projects and commentators present arguments about why so many people are leaving Christian institutions.

One of the concerns of church institutions is that people are claiming that their faith is "personal" and that Christianity is a "private faith." It's between me and Jesus.

Because their faith involves only them, people stay away from denominations and local church bodies. After all, their religion is between themselves and God.

Churches are quick to cite Hebrews 10:23—25 as biblical proof that Christians should be part of local church bodies:

> Let us hold fast to the confession of our hope without wavering, for He who promised is faithful; and let us consider how to stimulate one another to love and good deeds, not forsaking our own assembling together, as is the habit of some, but

> encouraging one another; and all the more as you see the day drawing near.[7]

A typical response to addressing the fact that people are leaving the church and staying home is to conclude they have a theological problem and that they simply need to be corrected with this passage in Hebrews.

However, what if people's departure from traditional church structures is less about doctrinal statements and more about *soil and roots*—deeply embedded Ideas in their hearts regarding their faith and views of reality?

Consider this: if we only preach the Gospel of Salvation but do not share the cosmic Gospel of the Kingdom, *we are promoting an Idea of a private faith.*

Western Christianity has, for decades, promoted a Gospel that focuses almost entirely on our personal relationship with Jesus. That Gospel has little or no impact on the three remaining relationships—with others, ourselves, or creation and culture.

If the point of the Gospel is to accept Jesus, live a decent life, and wait to escape the earth when we die, is there really a compelling reason to be a part of a church? Especially now, when we no longer need to attend a church to "be fed" through a sermon? We have access to hundreds of thousands of sermons from most teachers in the last century on our phones whenever we want.

This is the impact of Ideas. We spent the last century preaching a Gospel that focuses almost exclusively on a person's personal, private relationship with Jesus. And we've compounded that with an Idea system that suggests the body and the earth are "bad" and both need to be escaped.

If I have my ticket to heaven and my body and the world are wasting away anyhow, my primary reason for being involved in a Christian community is simply to learn how to evangelize more effectively so that others may be rescued from the inevitable demise of the earth.

If we fail to comprehend the fullness of the Gospel of the Kingdom, there is little need to become more like Jesus, to be discipled. We simply need to learn how to share the plan of salvation more effectively.

The Reductionist Gospel has had a profound impact on Western civilization in that many Christians have slowly receded from culture, having no vision or anticipation of culture being redeemed. In fact, we have unconsciously created two "realms"—the sacred and the secular.

Author and professor of religion at Redeemer University College Albert Wolters writes:

> This approach has led many Christians to abandon the "secular realm" to the trends and forces of secularism. Indeed, because of their two-realm theory, to a large degree, Christians have themselves to blame for the rapid secularization of the West. If political, industrial, artistic, and journalistic life, to mention only these areas, are branded as essentially "worldly," "secular," "profane," and part of the "natural domain of creaturely life," then is it surprising that Christians have not more effectively stemmed the tide of humanism in our culture?[8]

As we're beginning to uncover, Ideas have vast and sweeping consequences, for good or for evil. Our journey into Deep Discipleship depends on our ability to uncover and explore Ideas, both in the depths of our hearts and in culture. Otherwise, bad or incomplete Ideas lead to systemic problems.

In fact, the West is currently plagued by a few powerful problems that are wreaking havoc on the culture and the church. And all three problems are grounded in corrupted Ideas.

If we sense a disconnection between our spiritual life and the life the Bible reveals, and if we embrace the concept that this disconnection is grounded in Ideas in our hearts and in culture, let's now explore the three most pressing problems caused by faulty Ideas... and how to come together to solve them.

Chapter 4 Cumulative Key Takeaways

1. Though the Great Omission also has sweeping consequences for cultures and nations, individuals often experience a lack of discipleship as a disconnection from God, others, ourselves, and creation. We wonder if there is more to our life with God than what we're experiencing.
2. The "deep end of discipleship" occurs when we begin to explore the Ideas and desires that power and govern us.
3. An Idea is a fundamental concept, assumption, or principle in which our hearts are rooted but of which we are generally unaware.
4. An example of an Idea that has had far-reaching consequences in the last few hundred years is the Idea of the Gospel. What we currently assume as the Gospel is true, though incomplete. The clear Idea of the Gospel in the Bible is not simply our reconciliation to God, but the redemption and reconciliation of the entire cosmos through the power of the kingdom of God.

---

1. Mike McKinniss, "How God Became King: Kingdom and Cross, the Remaking of Meanings," *WordPress*, accessed October 20, 2023, https://mmckinniss.wordpress.com/2012/04/10/how-god-became-king-kingdom-and-cross-the-remaking-of-meanings/.
2. R. C. Sproul, "Essential Truths of the Christian Faith: The Kingdom of God," *BibleGateway*, accessed October 20, 2023, https://www.biblegateway.com/devotionals/essential-truths-of-the-christian-faith/2056/12/07.
3. Colossians 1:13–20

4. Corbett, S., & Fikkert, B. (2002). *When Helping Hurts* (pp. 32-33). Moody Publishers.
5. Jeremy Treat, "The One Thing Jesus Couldn't Stop Talking About," *FaithGateway*, accessed October 20, 2023, https://faithgateway.com/blogs/christian-books/the-one-thing-jesus-couldnt-stop-talking-about.
6. S. Michael Craven, "Recovering the Gospel of the Kingdom," *Breakpoint Colson Center*, accessed October 20, 2023, https://www.breakpoint.org/2019-01-recovering-the-gospel-of-the-kingdom/.
7. Hebrews 10:23–25
8. Wolters, A. (2005). *Creation Regained: Biblical Basics for a Reformational Worldview* (p. 65). William B. Eerdmans Publishing Company.

Part Two

The Three Primary Problems

Five
Uncovering The Problems

> We cannot solve our problems with the same thinking we used when we created them.
>
> —Albert Einstein[1]

Building on what we've explored about discipleship and Ideas, we now turn our attention to a rather bold (and most likely contested) claim: that the current state of Western culture and the church can be audaciously simplified down to Three Primary Problems, all of which are derived from incomplete, corrupted, or distorted Ideas that are widespread and pervasive.

Continuing the Story

I've been following Jesus since I was six years old, and I've been in church, studying the Bible, and involved in Christian service my entire life. Most of my career was in executive management, and half of that time was spent in full-time Christian ministry roles.

Though I had always believed I was a disciple of Jesus, the damage of the events I shared in the introduction drove me to become skeptical of the assumptions and facts I held dear. I was no longer sure if my perspective of my childhood faith was accurate, whether "rock solid" principles in my life were really all that solid, and who or what I could rely on.

And since disciple-making seemed to be central to Christianity, I questioned whether I really understood discipleship at all.

So, I went back to the beginning and asked two pivotal questions:

- What is a disciple, really?
- Was I truly one of them?

That was when I stumbled on the fact that discipleship is heart formation, spiritual formation, or even character formation. For some reason, despite being a part of Bible-believing churches my entire life, I never connected the dots that discipleship is a formative journey. I knew our hearts were changed at salvation. I guess I assumed discipleship was about growing as a Christian, but, at least for me, that growth unconsciously meant accumulating more knowledge about Jesus, Christianity, and the Bible.

What's stranger still is that I was aware of the concept of "sanctification," which is essentially the same thing as spiritual formation. And I knew that sanctification meant we were supposed to become "better people" as we grew in our knowledge of Jesus. I certainly hoped I would become a "better person" over the years despite having no vision or path for that journey.

For whatever reason, though, "spiritual formation" as the journey of discipleship finally made sense.

"Spiritual" refers to the core, the bedrock, the heart, and the roots of who we are. And "formation" is a journey familiar to us all, whether we recognize it or not, because we've all been formed in various ways throughout our lives.

Early childhood is the most formative time for everyone. However, we're also formed in the military, in college, in marriage, or through immersive experiences and communities such as competitive sports teams, sororities and fraternities, various camps, long-term mission trips, and so on.

All of these experiences are based on our desire to be formed to be more like someone else. Parents and caregivers make choices designed to form a toddler in the terrible twos into a mature and productive member of society. The military is designed to form a civilian into a soldier. College is specifically designed to receive a high school senior and form her into a successful and career-ready university graduate. Competitive sports teams are designed to break down the individual and merge him into a selfless member of a winning group, a team. Sororities and fraternities intentionally create formative cultures where those who rush become formed into people displaying the characteristics and goals of those societies.

We may have seen Michael Jordan play basketball and decided we wanted to "Be Like Mike." We wanted to be formed into him or someone just like him. Maybe as a kid, we idolized a parent or sibling or other relative, and we determined we wanted to grow up to become like that person.

When I was in my late twenties, I had a special opportunity to sit down and have a one-on-one lunch with John Bogle, the founder of an enormous investment company called Vanguard. He was an investment icon. I left the conversation deeply admiring some of his character traits, and I wanted to become more like him.

At the core of Deep Discipleship is the intense desire to become more like our Master. We don't apprentice with Him simply to know more *about* Him. We apprentice so that we do the things He does, desire the things He desires, and love the things He loves. So that His words become our words. So that His habits become our habits. So that we relate to God, ourselves, others, and creation the way He relates to God, us, Himself, and creation.

After discovering that real discipleship means formation, I read *Restoration of the Heart* and began to mull over the concept that "how" we become disciples is the progressive transformation of unconscious Ideas.

Initially, this seemed weird. I didn't ever recall reading about "Ideas" in the Bible. I had never been taught that, at the very bottom of my heart, these Ideas about God, myself, others, and the world were governing me and that some of them aligned with my faith, but many others did not. That many of the Ideas that powered me weren't actually in line with the stated beliefs I held so tightly.

However, once we begin to look for these hidden Ideas in ourselves, others, our churches, and the culture, we can't "un-see" them. And as A. W. Tozer said, the process of probing the world of Ideas in the heart is, in fact, painful.[2] Other authors and thinkers have called this exploration by different names: the inward journey or self-introspection. Our ancient church thinkers often referred to it as simply "contemplation."

I eventually embraced the existence and power of these unconscious Ideas, though doing so raised two questions I thought I had long ago answered. If Ideas sit at the bedrock of our hearts and drastically impact whom we relate to and how, then:

- Did I really know Jesus?
- Did I really know myself?

In fact, our journey of Deep Discipleship will be stunted if we don't sincerely and earnestly ask and answer these two questions.

Do I Really Know Jesus?

To answer the first question, I figured it made sense to spend far more time with Him.

Though the entire Bible points to Jesus, the stories of His earthly life are found in the Gospels, so I threw myself into those books. I read them repeatedly, placing myself into the stories. I visualized myself following Him around and watching Him as He interacted with people. I was there when He fed the five thousand and when He verbally sparred with the Pharisees. I sat as a bystander when He spoke with the woman at the well. I joined the crowd, screaming, "Crucify Him." I slowly walked with the men speaking with a resurrected Jesus they didn't recognize on the road to Emmaus.

And I discovered that, although I had been following Him for a few decades, I didn't really *know* Him all that well. I knew a lot *about* Him, and I had a relationship with Him, but it didn't seem like a particularly close relationship.

By the same token, I realized I didn't understand His kingdom all that well. The kingdom seemed to be a pervasive, if not primary, theme in the Bible, yet my understanding of His kingdom was cloudy at best. I began asking people around me about how they define Jesus's kingdom, and I received as many answers as the number of people I asked.

I was pretty sure I understood Jesus as Savior. Did I really understand Him as King? If my spiritual formation is about becoming more like Him, it seemed vital that I explore His comprehensive purpose, even if it didn't fully align with what I had been taught.

Then, I turned my attention to the second question.

Do I Really Know Myself?

If we embrace the concept that spiritual formation is the process of becoming like someone else, then it requires us to know two people really well: the object of our formation and the subject of our formation. To become like Jesus, we need to know Him well, and we need to know ourselves well.

If I want to "Be Like Mike," I certainly need to assess my current basketball skills (I have none), my work ethic, my willingness to practice, my attitude, my character, and whether I am surrounded by or have access to coaches who can guide me to become more like Mike.

If I want to become an investment guru like John Bogle, I should look at my own investment philosophy to see where I agree with him and where I don't. I should look at my investment practices to see if what I am doing lines up with what he is doing. I should learn Bogle's habits and perspectives and then compare those with my habits and perspectives.

In our postmodern churches, we tend to assume that we can have and develop a relationship with God apart from our relationship with others or even a deep understanding of ourselves.

But knowledge of self is important, if not central, to our discipleship. John Calvin wrote, "We cannot expect to know God fully if we are not willing to know ourselves, for one depends on the other."[3]

This is an often-overlooked principle. Our relationship with God depends on our relationship with ourselves, on our willingness to uncover and confront our own hearts, our Ideas, and our desires. In my search, it became apparent that our ability to deepen our relationship with God is dependent on our ability or willingness to deepen our understanding of ourselves. This means diving into our hearts to explore our stories, our desires, and our unconscious Ideas.

I had been in Bible-believing churches for my entire life and had never heard this. Instead, self-contemplation was generally condemned unless you needed counseling for some crisis. Self-exploration reeked of navel-gazing, selfishness, and potentially succumbing to the broader culture's obsession with self-worship. After all, Zach Williams repeatedly sings that the point is to be "A little more like Jesus, a little less like me."[4] We're supposed to die to ourselves, right? How could digging into our stories help us chart a course into Deep Discipleship going forward?

In retrospect, the areas of modern Christianity that downplay and reject the exploration of one's story are at odds with the general notion that we should all be students of history. We teach our children world history, Western history, and perhaps church history. We now have access to DNA testing that provides us with deeper insight and information about our family history.

Why are we urged to study and explore various areas of history? Because as Winston Churchill famously said, "Those that fail to learn from history are doomed to repeat it."[5]

Yet efforts to understand how our past impacts our present and future are often diminished if not accused of being in conflict with Scripture, including Paul's proclamation in Philippians:

> "...but one thing I do: forgetting what lies behind and reaching forward to what lies ahead, I press on toward the goal for the prize of the upward call of God in Christ Jesus."[6]

I had reached a dilemma. My historical Ideas of discipleship were insufficient and unclear. The journey into Deep Discipleship meant a deepening relationship with Jesus both as Savior *and* King, and it meant diving into my own heart.

Distilling the Problems

And so began my exploration of the Three Primary Problems.

1. To become more like Jesus requires understanding Him as both Savior and King. As I alluded to in Chapter 4, I struggled to understand Jesus as King. I'd forgotten about the kingdom.
2. If the point of Deep Discipleship is to become more like Jesus, I need to know Him, and I need to better know myself, my story, and the Ideas and desires in my heart. This sounded selfish and potentially a bit dangerous. This presented a dilemma.
3. My historical church experience provided little help in taking this journey. As I started to compare common formative experiences (such as early childhood, marriage, college, and the military), I found little in common between those immersive experiences and my rather fragmented, disintegrated, disconnected Christian life. There seemed to

> be a substantial gap between what our hearts desperately desire and need in order to be formed like Jesus and what many of us currently experience in our churches and institutions.

The Forgotten Kingdom. The Discipleship Dilemma. The Formation Gap. These are the Three Primary Problems.

It soon became evident that the Three Primary Problems were not simply my problems. Over and over again, my interactions with others revealed the lack of an accurate context for who Jesus is and what He's doing (the Forgotten Kingdom), the importance of knowing both Him and ourselves really well (the Discipleship Dilemma), and the need for specific communities and experiences designed to form us (the Formation Gap).

Not only are these problems limiting and wounding Christians, but they are also at the center of the cultural and moral slide. As the church goes, so goes the culture.

As we're about to discover, the Three Primary Problems are built on incomplete or corrupt Ideas that are, for the most part, hidden and unconscious, though extremely powerful. That's the bad news. The good news is that all three problems are entirely solvable, and the New Testament provides us with a blueprint to do so.

Let's dig in.

Chapter 5 Cumulative Key Takeaways

- A primary reason for our sense of disconnection and loneliness is the "Great Omission," a struggle to genuinely make people who live and love like Jesus.
- Somewhat surprisingly, we are governed and powered by Ideas (embedded, typically unconscious, experienced

assumptions about reality). To explore these Ideas for the purpose of becoming more like Christ is to engage in Deep Discipleship, the journey into Stages 4, 5, and 6 of our spiritual formation.

- Faulty, corrupt, incomplete, and hidden Ideas have caused the development of Three Primary Problems in the West: the Forgotten Kingdom, the Discipleship Dilemma, and the Formation Gap.
- If we're to become more like Jesus, we must recapture the understanding of who He is as King and what His kingdom is all about. Becoming more like Jesus also requires us to know our own hearts and the Ideas and desires that power us. Unfortunately, modern Christianity lacks communities that are specifically designed for this deep work, resulting in a gap in our formation journey.

---

1. Albert Einstein, *BrainyQuote*, accessed October 20, 2023, https://www.brainyquote.com/quotes/albert_einstein_121993.
2. Willard, D. (2002). *Renovation of the Heart: Putting on the Character of Christ* (p. 100). NavPress.
3. Thompson, C. (2015). *The Soul of Shame* (p. 108). Inter-Varsity Press.
4. Zach Williams, "Zach Williams - Less Like Me (Official Music Video)," *YouTube*, accessed October 20, 2023, https://www.youtube.com/watch?v=fkYL1b7MCEw.
5. Winston Churchill, "History Repeating," Liberal Arts.vt.edu, accessed November 5, 2023, https://liberalarts.vt.edu/magazine/2017/history-repeating.html.
6. Philippians 3:13–14

Six
The Forgotten Kingdom

> In the history of the Western church redemption has often been misunderstood to be salvation from the creation rather than salvation of the creation.
>
> —Michael W. Goheen[1]

As mentioned previously, I begin a Soil & Roots class by asking participants to individually answer these questions:

1. What is the Gospel?
2. What is thc kingdom?

When answering question #1, most people say something to the effect of, "The good news that Jesus came and died to save me from my sins."

When it comes to the second question, people provide a variety of answers:

"The kingdom is the church."

"The kingdom is a spiritual, invisible concept."

"The kingdom is just another word for heaven."

"The kingdom refers to a future state we haven't experienced yet."

As we explored in Chapter 4, understanding the Gospel requires us to embrace the kingdom. Because our unconscious Ideas about the kingdom have such a deep impact on how we function in the world, let's dig deeper into this assumption as our first Primary Problem.

The First Commission

Many Christians are familiar with the biblical concept of "commission." The word's meaning is found in the word itself: *co-mission*. A mission with someone else. A "cooperative mission."

Virtually every Christian is familiar with the Great Commission found in Matthew 18—20. Here it is again:

> And Jesus came and spoke to them, saying, "All authority has been given to Me in heaven and on earth. Go therefore and make disciples of all the nations, baptizing them in the name of the Father and of the Son and of the Holy Spirit, teaching them to observe all things that I have commanded you; and lo, I am with you always, even to the end of the age." Amen.[2]

It's our "cooperative mission" with Jesus in the making of disciples. As King, He has all authority over everything in heaven and earth. And, as He promises at the end of His commission, He will be *with* us every step of our journey.

However, many modern Christians aren't familiar with God's *first commission*.

Just as the Great Commission was the *very last* thing Jesus said to His followers before He ascended, God's first commission was the *very first* thing He said to humans upon creating us. We find the first commission, known sometimes as the Cultural Commission, in Genesis 1:

> Then God said, "Let Us make man in Our image, according to Our likeness; and let them rule over the fish of the sea and over the birds of the sky and over the cattle and over all the earth, and over every creeping thing that creeps on the earth." God created man in His own image, in the image of God He created him; male and female He created them. God blessed them; and God said to them, "Be fruitful and multiply, and fill the earth, and subdue it; and rule over the fish of the sea and over the birds of the sky and over every living thing that moves on the earth."[3]

God created the world and then handed over the responsibility for populating it and subduing it to mankind. Humans are to fill the earth and refine it, form it, mold it, and make it to the glory of its Creator. This is mankind's first commission, and we already see some "royal" language here. We are to rule, to reign.

We are vice-regents on behalf of God. We are, in effect, kings and queens ruling the earth on behalf of our cosmic King. God created a kingdom and honored us with the role of forming and refining it for mankind's goodness.

If you share with people today (including most Christians) that our initial purpose is to be rulers of the earth, forming it for everyone's goodness, chances are you'll get some blank stares.

Doomed to Failure?

Though most Christians believe Revelation 21:5, which declares that Christ will one day make "...all things new..." and that some future version of our eternal existence will be free from corruption, sin, and harm, there is substantial disagreement on what the journey of the created order will be between now and then. How is Christ's kingdom impacting the entire earth right now, if at all?

In fact, a very powerful Idea that has seeped into the hearts and minds of many Christians is that the earth is primarily bad and must be escaped. The earth is doomed to some form of destruction, so the primary role of the Christian is to share the Gospel of Salvation so that others may escape a corrupted and inescapably fallen planet. There is little point in "ruling the earth" if the earth is a metaphorical *Titanic*, so marred and wounded by evil that it will eventually be destroyed.

At Soil & Roots, we call this view "Christian Fatalism."

Christian Fatalism is a pervasive Idea that has a profound impact on how we view the world and function in it. It not only affects how individuals relate and operate, but it also influences entire cultures and nations.

However, considering God repeatedly called His creation "good" in Genesis 1 (including human beings), Christian Fatalism is a difficult Idea to reconcile. If God created the world "good," why do many in this generation expect God's good world to be inevitably annihilated or devastated, assuming it has become inescapably "bad"?

In other words, why are we comfortable with the growth and success of the second commission but not the first?

Commission Confusion

Some who are aware of the Cultural Commission argue that God's initial instructions to mankind no longer apply because of the inception of sin in Genesis 3. It has, in effect, expired.

However, God restates the same Cultural Commission to Noah *after* the flood:

> And God blessed Noah and his sons and said to them, "Be fruitful and multiply, and fill the earth. The fear of you and the terror of you will be on every beast of the earth and on

> every bird of the sky; with everything that creeps on the ground, and all the fish of the sea, into your hand they are given. Every moving thing that is alive shall be food for you; I give all to you, as I gave the green plant. Only you shall not eat flesh with its life, that is, its blood. Surely I will require your lifeblood; from every beast I will require it. And from every man, from every man's brother I will require the life of man. Whoever sheds man's blood, by man his blood shall be shed, for in the image of God He made man. As for you, be fruitful and multiply; populate the earth abundantly and multiply in it."[4]

And King David reminds us of the Cultural Commission in Psalm 8:

> When I consider Your heavens, the work of Your fingers, the moon and the stars, which You have ordained; What is man that You take thought of him, and the son of man that You care for him? Yet You have made him a little lower than God, and You crown him with glory and majesty! You make him to rule over the works of Your hands; You have put all things under his feet, all sheep and oxen, and also the beasts of the field, the birds of the heavens and the fish of the sea, whatever passes through the paths of thc scas.[5]

David uses explicitly regal and royal language to describe mankind and our role in ruling the earth on behalf of our Creator, words such as "crown," "majesty," "rule," and everything is "under our feet."

Yet, as noted, many Christians hold to the Idea that our attempts to steward and rule creation and culture are doomed to failure because the earth's destruction is inevitable. This means that if the Cultural Commission hasn't expired, it must be futile.

Logically, we must then ask ourselves a critical question: if the Cultural Commission is futile, is the Great Commission futile? If mankind must ultimately fail at ruling the earth on behalf of God, so it will be destroyed in wrath, why should we expect growth and success in making disciples on behalf of that same God?

Interestingly, I've yet to hear a church leader claim that the Great Commission will ultimately fail. We know not everyone will come to Christ, but we certainly hope that everyone will hear about Him and be invited into His kingdom. In fact, most Christians seem highly optimistic about the Great Commission. Simple data affirms their optimism as the number of Christians worldwide continues to grow.[6]

Perhaps an underlying reason why some Christians believe the Cultural Commission will fail has to do with recognizing man's sin and its corruptive effects. Like ancient Israel, we just can't seem to get our act together, and we'll prove that again and again as we watch the world fall apart.

However, this offers no explanation for why the Great Commission should work out any better (and seriously calls into question the purpose of the Holy Spirit). Sin is sin. Why should sin thwart the Cultural Commission but not the Great Commission?

Perhaps these two commissions are not nearly as far apart as we think. Perhaps God's very first instruction to mankind—to populate, rule, and subdue the earth for the good of mankind and for God's glory —is assumed and even embedded in the very last instruction Jesus gave to mankind. And perhaps this paints an even broader, more comprehensive picture of discipleship than what most of us are used to.

Perhaps a disciple is someone becoming more like the King in order to join with Him in the redemption and restoration *of the entire earth.*

The Kingdom Story in the Old Testament

Exploring the very first thing God says to mankind gives us a hint that the kingdom is a theme woven through the entire grand story of God and humanity found in the Bible. In a sense, God creates a beautiful new kingdom and invites His image-bearers (a term that has a touch of royalty to it) to rule and reign over it on His behalf. He extends an extraordinary amount of power and authority to mankind to mold and form His new world.

God placed Adam and Eve into four relationships: with God, with each other, with themselves, and with creation. In the garden, all of those relationships were grounded in love. Adam and Eve loved God, loved each other, loved themselves, and ruled and reigned creation.

In Genesis 3, Adam and Eve rejected God's divine reign and attempted to rule God's creation all on their own. All four of the healthy relationships God provided for mankind were broken. God's initial kingdom was marred by the rebellion of His crowning creation, and, by necessity, Adam and Eve were removed from the mountain garden and sent into the wilderness.

As a result of their rebellion, a new domain arose, the kingdom of darkness. And mankind spent the first part of Genesis proving how horrible we are at playing God in this destructive kingdom.

However, the Creator soon revealed more of His plan to rescue and redeem His creation. He deeply desires to be with His people, and He will not be denied. He still desires mankind to rule and reign with Him.

This new section of the kingdom story starts with just one family, started by Abraham and Sarah.

In Genesis 12, God spoke with Abram (not yet renamed):

> Go forth from your country, and from your relatives and from your father's house, to the land which I will show you; and I will make you a great nation, and I will bless you, and make your

> name great; and so you shall be a blessing; and I will bless those who bless you, and the one who curses you I will curse. And in you all the families of the earth will be blessed.[7]

In Genesis 17, God renamed Abraham and made a covenant with him:

> As for Me, behold, My covenant is with you, and you will be the father of a multitude of nations. No longer shall your name be called Abram, but your name shall be Abraham; for I will make you the father of a multitude of nations. I have made you exceedingly fruitful, and I will make nations of you, and kings will come forth from you.[8]

Notice God's promise that "kings will come forth from you." Once we begin to read Scripture with an eye toward the themes of kingdom, kings, regality, reigning, authority, and power, we begin to see the concept of the kingdom as a theme that weaves not only through the New Testament but the entire Bible.

God promised that Abraham would be the father of many nations, not just one. Yet Israel's history is filled with ups and downs, most of which prove mankind continually attempts to usurp God's reign in favor of our own, and it repeatedly results in war, harm, and destruction.

As Israel experienced its various travails, its people eventually desired a human king. In one of the more heartbreaking scenes of the Old Testament, the Israelites demanded that God be removed from His position as their king. When Samuel talked to God on their behalf:

> The Lord said to Samuel, "Listen to the voice of the people in regard to all that they say to you, for they have not rejected you, but they have rejected Me from being king over them."[9]

God granted their wish for a human king. Yet despite their efforts, the twelve tribes of Israel existed as a unified nation for only a brief time under King David and his son, Solomon. The kingdom split after Solomon's reign. Much of the Old Testament details the reigns of various kings (most of whom ruled poorly), such as the two books of Kings and Chronicles.

Mankind had yet to find a king who would reign justly and rightly. Even King David, a man after God's own heart, struggled to maintain his personal and regal integrity. Yet God continually expresses His intention to be with His people and to rule and reign with us.

God desired to be with mankind physically and personally in the Garden. Though mankind rebelled, God returned to be physically and personally with His people in the form of the Jewish Tabernacle, journeying with Israel as they wandered in the desert. When Israel settled in the promised land, He once again came to them in the temple. God's original plan to rule and reign with His creation was not to be thwarted, even if we kept foolishly resisting Him. Heaven continued to come down to earth.

The Kingdom Story in the New Testament

The theme of the kingdom and the temple come together powerfully and finally in the person of Jesus Christ.

Jesus is announced as the kingdom of God at hand, and John describes Him as heaven and earth permanently joined together: "And the Word became flesh, and dwelt among us, and we saw His glory, glory as of the only begotten from the Father, full of grace and truth."[10]

Fully God, fully man. The winds of heaven enjoined to the stuff of earth. He "dwelt among us." In other words, He "templed" among us.

God would not be denied being with us, ruling and reigning with us, so He became a human king Himself in what was the most extraordinary act of kindness in history. Unlike all the previous kings, this King had come to finally break the back of the domain of darkness and incept the new kingdom, though this King came in a very unexpected way and lived a very unexpected life.

While on earth, He showed us what it means to live well in our four relationships: to love God, to love others, to love ourselves, and to steward creation. And He secures His Kingship not by defeating His foes, but by dying for them.

He "ascends" to His rule on the cross. He is given a robe and a crown. His cross bears a sign that reads "King of the Jews" in three languages. Though not at all what we normally picture as a king, regal language and imagery are replete throughout the Gospel accounts and the Passion Week.[11]

Jesus deals a death blow to the domain of darkness by refusing to stay dead. His Father grants Him all authority over all of heaven and earth, the entire cosmos, both visible and invisible. This unexpected King, who was born in a smelly stable and died essentially naked and broken for His people, ascends to the position of the almighty ruler and King of the Cosmos.

When He's finished His mission, He will return the kingdom to God the Father.

> For as in Adam all die, so also in Christ all will be made alive. But each in his own order: Christ the first fruits, after that those who are Christ's at His coming, then comes the end, when He hands over the kingdom to the God and Father, when He has abolished all rule and all authority and power. For He must reign until He has put all His enemies under His feet.[12]

And for whatever reason, this new King didn't fully consummate His Kingdom of Light on His first trip here. He's going to do that on His second trip. So, His kingdom is "both here and not yet fully here." This new kingdom, this new reality, is so radically different from the domain of darkness that we often struggle to get our arms around it.

The Magnificent Seven

As Dr. Jeremy Treat writes, the kingdom is "God's reign through God's people over God's place."

The kingdom of God is the in-breaking of God Himself into a world confused and wounded by darkness, and the King is, right now, reclaiming and redeeming what is rightfully His, which means everything.

Here are just seven characteristics of the kingdom:

1. This kingdom began with the arrival of the King.

2. The King is also the Key. In Colossians 1, Paul says we are transferred from the domain of darkness to the kingdom of God through our redemption in Christ.

3. The kingdom is already here, but also not yet. Jesus came and incepted the kingdom but has not yet fully consummated it. We are in this middle ground, this in-between period. So we are here in the kingdom, but Jesus has not yet finalized its overwhelming conquering of the kingdom of darkness.

4. The kingdom is cosmic in scope. It redeems all four of man's primary relationships: with God, ourselves, others, and with creation and culture.

One sub-point on this. Some people's Idea of the kingdom of light is that it refers to the church, the people who genuinely follow Jesus. The church is part of the kingdom and the heralds of it, but the kingdom is vastly larger than the church. We find this spelled out in the Colossians 1 passage we've been exploring.

Paul explains that Christ is ruling over everything, and then he says that Christ is *also* head of the body, the church. He considers the kingdom and the church two separate things. The church is part of the kingdom and has a crucial role in the kingdom's expansion, but the church is not the same thing as the kingdom.

5. The kingdom is both spiritual and physical. Much like the fact that many people assume the kingdom only means the church, many people hold to the Idea that the kingdom is only spiritual. It's solely about the transformation of the heart, and so it's only invisible.

Again, we find "reduction" here. The Gospel of Salvation is true, but is a reduction of the Gospel of the Kingdom. The church is part of the kingdom, but it is only a part. The kingdom certainly is spiritual, but it's not only spiritual. It's also physical. It must be both.

There are numerous examples of spiritual transformation resulting in physical transformation in the Bible. Let's consider Zacchaeus in Luke 19:1—10.

Zacchaeus climbs the tree and spots Jesus, who tells Him He's coming to his house. Zacchaeus has an encounter with Jesus Christ, and what is the first thing that Zacchaeus does? He makes economic restitution to the people he's cheated. He makes physical changes in the physical world (the exchange of money) because of his spiritual transformation.

When we choose to stop following ourselves and instead turn and follow the King, we make all sorts of changes to the physical world as a result of our inner transformation.

At the birth of the church in Acts 2, people began selling their property and possessions and were sharing them with those in need. In Acts 6, we see the early church making provisions for widows who were being neglected. Church history is filled with story after story of people who made small and large changes to the physical world because of their spiritual, invisible formation. Spiritual transformation has been at the heart of both small and massive restorations of marriages, families, communities, media, the arts, governments, economies, education, justice, and social and racial inequities.

6. The kingdom of God is growing.

There are three parables in Mark 4, where Jesus specifically outlines the growth and progression of the kingdom of God.

In the Parable of the Sower, He describes the kingdom as the good seed yielding a 30-, 60-, or 100-fold harvest.

In the Parable of the Seed, the kingdom sprouts up overnight.

And in the third parable, the Parable of the Mustard Seed, Christ says:

"How shall we picture the kingdom of God, or by what parable shall we present it? It is like a mustard seed, which, when sown upon the soil, though it is smaller than all the seeds that are upon the soil, yet when it is sown, it grows up and becomes larger than all the garden plants and forms large branches; so that the birds of the air can nest under its shade."

The kingdom is growing and can't be stopped.

7. The kingdom of God is greater than the kingdom of darkness.

This is another characteristic of the kingdom that doesn't always seep into our hearts. This conflict between the two kingdoms is not *Star Wars*. There is no Force. There is no balance between good and evil. There is no yin and yang.

Jesus Christ and His kingdom are greater than the kingdom of darkness.

There's a passage in which Jesus is casting out demons, and the Pharisees accuse Jesus of casting them out by the power of Satan. Jesus responds in Luke 11:20—22:

> But if I cast out demons by the finger of God, then the kingdom of God has come upon you. When a strong man, fully armed, guards his own house, his possessions are undisturbed. But when someone stronger than he attacks him and overpowers him, he takes away from him all his armor on which he had relied and distributes his plunder.

It's difficult to read this passage as anything else but Jesus taking a shot at the kingdom of darkness. Jesus, the stronger man, is binding the darkness and plundering it. He's come to take His stuff back. And that's what He's been doing ever since.

How Does the Kingdom Grow?

While we await the final consummation of the kingdom, how does it grow? Jesus incepted it with His arrival on earth, taught about it constantly during His ministry, repeatedly asserted the kingdom would grow without fail (Mark 3:22—27, Mark 4:26—34), secured it when He died and was resurrected, and assumed His rightful role as King of it when He ascended. But in this in-between time, how does His kingdom expand?

God's *first* commission to mankind was to fill the earth and rule it on behalf of our Creator. His *second* commission envelops the first and explains how God's new reality grows in a world still struggling with sin and death.

The second commission invites us to make followers, apprentices of our ascended King, who are welcomed into the community of the new kingdom and who learn and study everything Jesus taught *so that we become more like our King and do the things He did.* Once again, we are commissioned to be vice-regents on behalf of the ruler of the universe and to expand His kingdom. We are called to be disciples.

Just as Jesus did, we are called to reconnect, restore, redeem, re-integrate, and recreate.

This Idea of the kingdom is in stark contrast to the modern-day Idea of church growth. It is the difference between an underlying Idea that the earth is something to be escaped and the Idea that the earth is something to be restored. If our unconscious Idea is to escape a "bad" creation, our focus will be on evangelism and relief efforts. If our unconscious Idea is to restore and redeem a good creation that an already defeated dark kingdom has besieged, we not only evangelize and relieve, but we also operate on the premise that creation and all seven mountains of culture are ripe for Ideas of light, Ideas that bring goodness, beauty, and human flourishing.

The kingdom of light grows through the making of disciples. We do the things our King did. If this sounds oddly similar to the *first* commission's command "to multiply and steward the earth," we're onto something.

The Forgotten Kingdom: Bad Body, Bad World

If we are to become more like Jesus, we need to understand Him as both Savior and King. If our Idea of Him does not include Him as our current cosmic King and we neglect the fact He has come to redeem everything, we face downstream, distorted consequences.

Let's just take a look at one.

Many Westerners tend to consciously or unconsciously embrace the Idea that the physical body and the world are both "bad."

Some time ago, I heard an evangelical leader claim that life is purely spiritual and the body is corrupt and dying. We can't trust or pay attention to our bodies because they're sinful. It's the spirit that remains, so ignore the body. And the earth is inherently bad, so the purpose of evangelism is to help people escape the earth.

That's simply not true. God made all creation good (including the body), and our purpose is not to escape it. Some claim that, although God created everything good, sin has essentially made everything irredeemably "bad." However, Paul reasserts the innate "goodness" of creation in 1 Timothy:

> For everything created by God is good, and nothing is to be rejected if it is received with gratitude; for it is sanctified by means of the word of God and prayer.[13]

We are embodied souls. We are unified beings. The body was created good, and the only reason this version wastes away and dies is because of sin, not because of God's original design. This is why understanding creation is so essential to the Gospel. Your body is a gift from God.

All of us in Christ will one day have glorified, eternal physical bodies. We started out as embodied souls, and we will spend eternity as... embodied souls.

To claim the body is somehow evil or bad is part of a system called Gnosticism, not biblical Christianity. Gnosticism devalues the physical in favor of the spiritual. The Bible does not agree.

Our final destination is not a disconnected, ethereal plane. It's heaven and earth rejoined. Jesus Himself is the foretaste of our future reality, the new heaven and the new earth as one place.[14] So, the point isn't to escape the earth. It's to redeem it, to restore it.

It's ironic that so many hold to the Idea that the body and the earth are bad. Not only did God pronounce them both good, but the King of the Cosmos is a human being with *a body*, and He came *to save the earth*, not to escape it.

This is why solving this Primary Problem, the Forgotten Kingdom, is so vital. If the point of being a disciple is to become more like Jesus, that doesn't simply include His characteristics, such as the fruits of the Spirit, sacrifice, and wisdom. It means we embrace His purpose, His mission. His mission is the already-but-not-yet kingdom. If we don't understand and embrace Jesus as the conquering King of the Universe who is, right now, putting all enemies under His feet as He grows His church, we will struggle mightily in our journey to become more like Him. And we'll miss out on the cosmic redemption He is, right now, accomplishing.

If we fail to understand His purpose and His mission, we unwittingly divorce ourselves from His work in creation and culture. Instead of viewing ourselves as the rightful rulers of creation, we recede from beautifying, resourcing, and sustaining the earth. We might reasonably ask why so few of the voices calling for the care and maintenance of the earth are Christian. We have ceded virtually all of that work to people working from an entirely different worldview. However, our reluctance to care for God's creation is understandable if we assume its future is utter destruction. This is a mistake and a rejection of the Cultural Commission.

In generations past, God's presence in the redemption and restoration of the seven mountains was assumed and expected. The Middle Ages brought extraordinary formation and transformation to education, media, the arts, governmental philosophy, science, and business. Again, because the underlying Ideas in modern Christianity suggest separating from the mountains of culture instead of engaging them, the Ideas of darkness have gained footholds. These are not the Ideas that should govern a people whose King is "making all things new."

The kingdom is certainly "God's reign through God's people over God's place." This kingdom of light, however, is also energetic, advancing, and powerful. It has already defeated the kingdom of darkness, and the King, by His own pronouncement, is plundering what the darkness has stolen, bringing redemption, restoration, and healing to every corner of the earth.

As apprentices of Jesus for the purpose of becoming more like Him, is this the Idea of His kingdom that our hearts embrace?

Chapter 6 Cumulative Key Takeaways

1. Somewhat surprisingly, we are governed and powered by Ideas (embedded, typically unconscious assumptions about reality). To explore these Ideas for the purpose of becoming

more like Christ is to engage in Deep Discipleship, the journey into Stages 4, 5, and 6 of our spiritual formation.

2. Incorrect or faulty Ideas are at the heart of the Three Primary Problems facing the West today. The first of these, the Forgotten Kingdom, has caused numerous dangerous and downstream consequences. We have reduced Jesus to simply our personal Savior and His kingdom to nebulous or ambiguous concepts of the church or something purely spiritual. Rather, Jesus is the reigning King of the Cosmos, and His kingdom includes every speck of the universe. Modern Christians often have little vision for the reformation of all of creation and culture. In fact, the church has often withdrawn from both, yet Deep Discipleship involves embracing Jesus's cosmic work.

---

1. Michael W. Goheen, *Mission Worldview*, MissionWorldView.com, accessed November 5, 2023, https://missionworldview.com/wp-content/uploads/2020/06/ea8a85_b2ec6ee9209548219dc3aca350c9a47f.pdf.
2. NKJV.
3. Genesis 1:26–28
4. Genesis 9:1–7
5. Psalm 8:3–8
6. "Christianity by Country," Wikipedia.com, accessed November 7, 2023, https://en.wikipedia.org/wiki/Christianity_by_country.
7. Genesis 12:1–3
8. Genesis 17:4–6
9. 1 Samuel 8:7
10. John 1:14
11. Passion Week refers to the week between Palm Sunday and Easter Sunday, also known as "Holy Week."
12. 1 Corinthians 15:22–25
13. 1 Timothy 4:4–5
14. Isaiah 65:17, 2 Peter 3:12–13, Revelation 21, 22.

Seven
The Discipleship Dilemma

> The purpose in a man's heart is like deep water, but a man of understanding will draw it out.
> —The Book of Proverbs[1]

To cultivate Deep Discipleship, we journey together to focus our lives on becoming like Jesus, though we are born into an era plagued by Three Primary Problems.

As we've discovered, the Forgotten Kingdom presents an immediate problem. While we may be familiar with knowing Jesus as our Savior and our friend, we will struggle to become more like Him if we don't also comprehend His Kingship and His growing kingdom. If we don't grasp the fullness of His cosmic purpose and plan, we won't fully grasp our own role within them.

Also, becoming like someone else requires us to know two people well: the object of our formation and the subject of our formation. So, in addition to needing to know Jesus fully, we need to grow in the understanding of our own hearts; that is, we need to explore the Ideas and desires that power and govern us.

As Christians, this journey to understand our own hearts may be challenged by our theological notions. We may have latched onto the verse from Jeremiah 17:9 that in the *New American Standard Version* calls our hearts "desperately sick" and asks, "Who can understand it?" We may well wonder: are we able to discern our hearts with any integrity? If so, can we actually discover the Ideas and desires that power us with any clarity?

We may be, in fact, facing a dilemma: the Discipleship Dilemma. If we are to be formed more like Jesus, we not only need to know Him, but we also need to come to understand our own soil and roots—yet digging beneath the surface to uncover these hidden Ideas and desires is unconventional in Christian circles.

And so, I set about interviewing friends, family, pastors, and counselors while also diving into a library of books ranging in topics from theology to education, from therapy to trauma, and from neuroscience to human relationships.

My intent was to answer two central questions:

- Is it possible to explore our hearts in order to uncover the Ideas and desires that govern us?
- If so, how?

The answer to the first question is yes; it is happily possible to uncover hidden Ideas and desires in our hearts. In fact, God is constantly inviting us into that exploration to experience His healing and freedom.

The answer to the second question is another term that may be unfamiliar to you. It's a process, or perhaps a habit, we call "Heartview."

An Introduction to Heartview

The Bible provides ample evidence and instruction about how we may peer into the recesses of our hearts as we journey through Deep Discipleship.

It teaches that our hearts consistently and inevitably reveal the Ideas and desires that sit at the bedrock of our soils if we are paying close attention. And if we are courageously curious about ourselves and God, we'll uncover tremendous insight into the actual condition of our hearts versus what our polite interactions display.

This process of Heartview involves evaluating and exploring the "Eight Indicators" that God has wired into every human being. The Eight Indicators are our thoughts, emotions, health, behaviors, relationships, words, and stewardship of time and money.

Regardless of how we present ourselves on the surface, our hearts will always bubble up their true Ideas and desires through these Eight Indicators.

These indicators are powerful tools as we journey into Deep Discipleship. Working through our indicators leads to wonderful and freeing steps forward as we seek to do the things Jesus did.

Uncover. Determine. Immerse.

Heartview is a simple, ongoing, three-step process in which we engage with God and a trusted friend or two:

1. Uncover. We use our Eight Indicators to *uncover* our hidden Ideas and desires in cooperation with God and trusted, safe friends.
2. Determine. We *determine* whether our Ideas bend toward the kingdom of darkness or the kingdom of light.
3. Immerse. We *immerse* ourselves in cultures designed to transform dark Ideas into light.

This may sound unique, yet we naturally engage in this type of process all the time.

Let's say you *uncover* the fact that you can only type ten words per minute on your computer. Because you work on your computer every day, your boss helps you *determine* that typing only ten words per minute is "bad." It negatively impacts your work. So, you *immerse* yourself in a culture designed to transform your typing deficiency into a honed skill. You invest time in relevant typing courses, and you begin to develop good typing habits. With enough practice, instruction, and encouragement in the right environment, pretty soon, you're zooming along at 70 words per minute.

Heartview applies these three steps to the most vital formative experience of our lives. Spiritual formation is a lifelong journey, so Heartview should be practiced slowly, patiently, and gently.

Heartview embraces courage, kindness, and curiosity. It is easy to understand, but it may be difficult to do. And it may be painful. Heartview not only means evaluating Ideas from creation and culture, but it also means digging into our personal, individual stories. It means understanding our families of origin and early childhood experiences to grasp how the Ideas in our Soil were originally formed and how they influence us today.

Also, it's important to remember that God has placed us into four relationships: with Him, with others, with ourselves, and with creation and culture. The Gospel of the Kingdom proclaims that our King is redeeming and reconciling all four relationships, so Heartview explores each indicator considering all four relationships.

Before we dig in, it's also vital to note that Jesus is the only human being who is fully integrated and wholly unified in His Ideas and indicators. His thoughts, emotions, physical state, actions, relationships, words, and use of time and money perfectly reflect and embody only Ideas of light.

To varying degrees, the rest of us are all somewhat disintegrated: our Ideas and desires don't always align with our beliefs, and it's difficult to precisely determine the connection between our hearts and our indicators. That's okay. We are all humans in progress.

When we practice Heartview, we will encounter our own sins and (very importantly) *the sins committed against us.* Because many of the Ideas and desires that govern us were formed by our relationships with others, it's important to practice Heartview with gentleness, candor, and a willingness to name people, actions, relationships, and sins for what they are.

Because this book is a primer of sorts, we will not be diving into each indicator in detail. My purpose over the next two chapters is to give you a general overview of each indicator and to go deeper into just one or two.

However, the *Soil & Roots* podcast features an entire season on Heartview and all Eight Indicators, so feel free to listen to those episodes if you want to explore further.[2]

Thoughts

In 1637, philosopher and scientist René Descartes famously said, "I think; therefore I am," and his statement has become a bedrock assumption of much of Western philosophy and culture, including the church.[3] Many people function from the assumption that we are what we think. We are far more complex than that, but our thought patterns are an indicator to help us uncover the Ideas and desires in our soils.

So, what *is* thinking? Here's a simple definition:

> It is the activity of searching out what *must* be true, or *cannot* be true, in the light of given facts or assumptions.[4]

Notice how the definition qualifies this activity or search for truth—it's based on given facts or assumptions. Remember how we define Ideas: "fundamental concepts, principles, and assumptions." So, our

Ideas are directly intertwined with our thoughts. Our Ideas drive and govern our thoughts. In some way, our Ideas sit underneath our thoughts.

One of the most quoted verses in the Bible about thoughts is from Proverbs:

> Do not eat the bread of a selfish man, or desire his delicacies; for as he thinks within himself, so he is. He says to you, "Eat and drink!" but his heart is not with you. You will vomit up the morsel you have eaten, and waste your compliments.[5]

Let's note the phrase we commonly hear in sermons: "as a man thinks within himself, so he is." Our internal thoughts point us to our core, our hearts. That's why "Thoughts" is our first Idea Indicator. What and how we think uncovers our true selves, our true desires, and what we love, as well as our hidden Ideas.

Human beings have a unique ability called "metacognition." We have the ability to think about what we think about! That's the essence of evaluating our thoughts as a Heartview Indicator—developing the habit of asking ourselves *why* we think the thoughts we do. What's underneath our thought patterns? We *uncover* the *why* behind our thoughts, *determine* if our *why* is from the kingdom of light or darkness, and then *immerse* ourselves in a culture that will help us transform our thoughts from darkness to light.

Here's a simple example. Consider a woman who privately struggles to think of herself as beautiful. When she thinks about herself or talks to herself, she typically doesn't address herself as someone who is made in the image of God and is, therefore, beautiful. She often thinks she doesn't measure up to some standard, or she fears how people perceive her. She thinks negatively of herself for not being a certain height or weight or shape or body condition, and she's constantly comparing herself to the current culture's Ideas of physical beauty.

However, she may have never stopped to think about *why* she thinks of herself as someone who isn't beautiful. Her courageous step forward is to *uncover* the Ideas that drive her thought patterns. Why does she not think of herself as a handcrafted work of a divine artist, singularly unique and beautiful?

That's the uncovering stage. Chances are her unconscious Ideas of beauty were developed as part of her personal story. She was immersed in a culture of formation when she was a child, and her family may not have considered her to be beautiful. Or she was only beautiful when she performed a certain way or did certain things. Or someone she trusted used her or exploited her, and her Ideas of beauty became damaged and corrupted. Or she made some unfortunate decisions, and she doesn't think she deserves to be considered beautiful.

Once she's *uncovered* the "why," the next step is to *determine* if her Ideas come from the kingdom of darkness or the kingdom of light. Obviously, if her thought patterns reveal she doesn't think of herself as an amazing, beautiful work of art, her Ideas of beauty are from the kingdom of darkness.

The best way for her to transform a dark Idea into a light Idea is to immerse herself in a culture that slowly and sacrificially reinforces truthful Ideas of beauty. And this usually happens over long periods by engaging in intentional habits that reinforce life-giving Ideas of beauty, particularly among intimate relationships with God, family members, and friends, all in a community that experiences her as she should be experienced.

One of the most powerful Scripture references endorsing the practice of evaluating our thoughts with God is found in Psalm 139:

> Search me, O God, and know my heart; try me and know my anxious thoughts; And see if there be any hurtful way in me and lead me in the everlasting way.[6]

Emotions

Many years ago, my wife, Jessica, walked into our tiny living room where I sat, and she was grinning from ear to ear. She was holding a pregnancy test, and it was positive. We were going to have another baby. Our son, Caleb, was going to have a little brother or sister.

We were overjoyed.

We waited a few weeks to share the news, and then my creative wife came up with a crafty way to tell our families that she was pregnant. They were all thrilled, and we began preparing for our new baby. But just a day or so later, something went wrong. What appeared to be a healthy pregnancy turned out to be unhealthy, and within a week or two, our baby was gone. Jessica suffered a miscarriage.

Though the shock and grief of the miscarriage were terrible, what struck us was the response from other Christians.

The statute of limitations for grieving a miscarriage in a Christian community is apparently about a week and a half. After that, we realized that everyone else had moved on, and we had better move on as well; otherwise, it might look like we lacked faith in God. About four weeks after the miscarriage, I brought it up to a close friend. He looked at me incredulously and asked in all seriousness, "Why are you guys still upset about this?"

Jessica and I have rarely spoken about our baby in public since. Yet it's been over twenty years, and on many days, maybe most days, I still think about our child. I imagine our baby is a girl, and I miss her. I long for her. I want to meet her. I know someday I will, though I still feel the grief. I still feel the loss, even decades later.

Am I allowed to feel this way? Aren't I supposed to just feel joyful? Aren't I supposed to trust in God and happily look forward to that day when I meet my daughter on the other side? Why should I still be sad?

Let's explore just two questions about feelings (I use the terms feelings and emotions synonymously):

- What is the role of emotions in the life of a person who follows Jesus?
- What may we learn by paying attention to them?

1. What is the Role of Emotions for the Person Who Wants to Become More Like Jesus?

The Christian life is filled with paradoxes. One definition states: "Paradox is a noun defined as a seemingly absurd or self-contradictory statement or proposition that, when investigated or explained, may prove to be well-founded or true."[7] So, it's something that, on the surface, appears to be impossible or contradictory, but still can be held together, even if we don't understand how.

The role of our emotions often seems like a paradox. On the one hand, we think that too many people are ruled by their emotions. They are governed by their feelings. Their lives are ordered around things that make them feel a certain way. This may be the Christian who jumps from conference to conference, from emotional service to emotional service, always seeking a sensual high from some sort of ecstatic spiritual experience. Or it may be the person who uses various types of addictions to numb their pain or replace it with drug-induced happiness. Or the thrill-seeker and adrenaline junkie who wants to feel the exhilaration of conquering some sort of physical adventure or business acquisition, and they get depressed when they aren't overcoming something.

On the other hand, there are people who consciously or unconsciously believe that most emotions are bad or wrong—that a good Christian is calm, peaceful, tranquil, and even-tempered all the time. They quote Galatians 5 and extol the fruits of the spirit, though they neglect to talk about Jesus making a whip and overturning the tables in the temple, intentionally insulting the Pharisees, and getting irritated with His disciples. These Christians generally consider what they deem to be "negative" emotions to be signs of an immature Christian, or they think feelings are more related to personality than to character. "Some people are just more emotional than others," they might say.

Certainly, we may struggle to control our emotions at times, or perhaps we struggle to feel at all. However, struggling to control our emotions or struggling to have emotions doesn't invalidate emotions. God created us with feelings. They are part of His design for humanity, and they are part of the human experience.

Since Deep Discipleship is about becoming more like Jesus, let's look to Him to determine what role emotions play in the life of a Christian. From what we learn about Jesus in the Gospels, does He feel? Does He express emotion? Does He fit the picture of an unfeeling, almost passive person who brushes things off with a polite word about God's goodness, or does He show us His heart by showing us His emotions?

How about anger? Jesus got angry more than once. He expressed his anger, and in a few instances, He showed it physically. Jesus became visibly angry at certain injustices.

Grief? Jesus wept at the death of Lazarus, even though He was moments away from raising His friend from the dead. Matthew tells us Jesus was so intensely grieved and distressed in the garden before His betrayal that it had a physical impact on His body.

Sadness? Jesus expressed sadness. He was sad over the future of Israel; He was sad at the sin and death in the world.

Happiness? Joy? Loneliness? Yes, on all counts.

Jesus is a deeply emotional man, and He was free to express those emotions when He walked the earth. Jesus committed no sin, yet He expressed all the emotions we just noted and more. He is the most human human ever to walk the earth, and He was a man of deep and expressive feelings.

If we want to become more like Jesus, and if we want our hearts to embody the Ideas and desires of Jesus, then we should expect to likewise become people of deep and expressive emotions. At times, that may mean expressing anger, grief, sadness, and loneliness, along with happiness, joy, gladness, and wonder.

Emotions tend to work like water in a pressurized tank. They're going to find their way out one way or the other. It's better to express them while digging under the surface to uncover what they're telling us now versus bottling them up or ignoring them and suffering later on.

2. What May We Learn by Uncovering the "Why" Underneath Our Emotions?

Neuroscientist Curt Thompson wrote, "Remember that emotion is not a debatable phenomenon. It is an authentic reflection of our subjective experience, one that is best served by attending to it."[8]

Author and counselor Dr. Chip Dodd argues that emotions and feelings are signposts that point us back to the depths of our hearts and our stories. We can develop the skill of learning to discern the Ideas and desires in our hearts if we pay attention to our feelings.

He writes, "Feelings help us name what we are experiencing in our hearts. Feelings bring us to the confession of how wonderfully frightening it is to live the mystery of being with God and others."[9]

An example of how we might identify an emotion as an indicator of a deeper reality is found in a condition we rarely discuss in church: rage.

David Damico agrees that it's vital we pay attention to our emotions in his surprisingly titled book, *Faces of Rage.*

> Rage is as ordinary as the common cold, and neither vows of self-control nor confessing the name of Jesus in militaristic determination will effect a lasting cure. Rage must be pulled out by its roots—and its roots are buried deep in the painful territory of unresolved loss that most of us don't care to visit.[10]

Rage, according to Damico, is not the red-faced, explosive response we tend to think of. Instead, it's the result of NOT dealing with loss. He defines rage as:

> [T]he escape routes from dealing with our real feelings connected with real losses—no matter how insignificant. When we spend our lives consciously or unconsciously avoiding loss, we aren't available for meaningful relationships—not with others, ourselves, or even God. In essence, rage is a self-protective shield we use to avoid loss-threatening circumstances or events... Rage's sole purpose is to keep us from resolving loss, which would free us to love and experience life in the present.[11]

Rage may take many forms, and many of them aren't always self-evident: controlling behavior, workaholism, emotional distance and difficulty forming true, intimate relationships, emotional numbness, and insecurities about money. We may appear as wonderful, calm, peaceful Christian men or women on the outside and still be plagued by rage on the inside—the suppression of unresolved loss. Rage corrupts the Ideas in our hearts, particularly core Ideas like identity, value, power, purpose, and love.

Some of us are reluctant to talk about rage because we don't want to talk about unresolved loss, at least not in church. If we don't get that job we wanted, we say it's God's will. If we are struck with an illness, we remind our friends that God is the Great Physician. If our marriage is loveless and routine, we remind ourselves that the joy of the Lord is our strength.

We may even feel guilty if we confess our sadness at having our hearts broken or our desires unmet. Yet we serve a God who prefers we come to Him honestly and openly versus offering our church-approved platitudes.

As Chip Dodd concludes, "...we have been taught to associate feelings with moral judgments against ourselves and others, rather than recognizing true feelings as created with us to allow us to face ourselves."[12]

Health

There's a fascinating verse in Proverbs 3 that reads:

> Do not be wise in your own eyes; fear the Lord and turn away from evil. It will be healing to your body and refreshment to your bones.[13]

In fact, Proverbs contains several passages that connect our spiritual, invisible, internal condition to physical or mental health:

> A joyful heart is good medicine, but a broken spirit dries up the bones.[14]
>
> Pleasant words are a honeycomb, sweet to the soul and healing to the bones.[15]
>
> My son, give attention to my words; incline your ear to my sayings. Do not let them depart from your sight; keep them in the midst of your heart. For they are life to those who find them and health to all their body.[16]

In his third epistle, the apostle John writes to Gaius and opens with:

> Beloved, I pray that in all respects you may prosper and be in good health, just as your soul prospers.[17]

Paul tells the Corinthians that the body is the "temple of the Holy Spirit," the physical and spiritual existing together. We are not a spirit *with* a body—we are embodied souls. We are integrated beings. Our spiritual condition impacts our physical health and vice versa.

Let's walk through a few points about health as a Heartview Indicator.

Every cold, sickness, or injury we experience is NOT a sign of the Ideas and desires in our hearts. If you fall off your bike and break your arm, that's not going to tell you much about what you love or your unconscious Ideas. In a sinful and broken world, we're all susceptible to harm. Neither is every illness or tragedy the consequence of that individual's sin or wrong choices. You may remember that when the disciples asked Jesus about a certain blind man, they assumed that the man was born blind because of some sin in his family history. Jesus assured them that wasn't the case.

However, numerous physical and mental illnesses may, in some cases, be traced to spiritual conditions. Depression, anxiety, fatigue, headaches, body pains, and other symptoms all have potential interconnections with our spiritual state. The loss of hope can have a devastating impact on mental and physical health. So can grief, loneliness, and betrayal. And some of those conditions stretch far back into our stories.

It's important that we carefully assess our overall health and not neglect our hearts or spirits. What are we addicted to and why? If we're constantly tired and there's no good physical explanation, what might our hearts be telling us? Is our heart weighed down and wounded? Is our rage or anxiety seeping out through our bodies, through our physical health?

If we suffer from anxiety or depression and it's harming us

physically, might we consider venturing into the deep waters of our hearts with someone trained to understand and walk with us through our stories? Could certain challenges with physical or mental health actually be signs of a spiritual condition, and are we listening carefully to what our hearts may be communicating through the Heartview Indicator of our health?

I am grateful for doctors, counselors, therapists, and all the others who work to bring health and harmony to the body and mind. These are highly important and needed vocations, and God gives wisdom and knowledge to humanity to be used for our good in a variety of ways. But we should not segment the mind, body, and spirit, treating them as if they are distinct from one another; we should rather view ourselves as unified, integrated beings, as God made us. That may mean we need to dive into our personal stories and the Ideas in our hearts to understand our health in all its facets.

Behaviors

Our behaviors are amazingly helpful indicators pointing to the Ideas and desires in our hearts.

Let's use this definition: a behavior is a repeated pattern of how a person acts in relation to God, others, self, and creation.

Dark Behavioral Formation

Numerous articles and documentaries have been produced about one of the most notorious men in recent American history—Hugh Hefner, the founder of *Playboy*. He was masterful at understanding and exploiting human behavior, particularly that of young women. He used his extraordinary wealth and privilege to seduce and groom young women for his own purposes. When it came to his core Ideas of value, power, purpose, and love, he viewed young women as meat for him to enjoy and profit from at his discretion. He considered himself a god, and he used and abused his victims as he saw fit.

Likewise fascinating (and sad) are the stories of some of the abused women at the Playboy Mansion.

The streaming service Hulu released a sobering documentary about Hefner called "The Secrets of Playboy." In it, they report that Hefner targeted certain types of young women in his operation, those with a "girl next door" persona. As we noted, our family of origin is incredibly powerful in framing our heart's Ideas, and many of the targeted women who came into Hefner's web had tragic origin stories. Stories of absent or abusive fathers, sexual abuse, and legalistic, controlling homes were common.

These victims were enthralled by the money, power, and allure of life at the Playboy Mansion, and Hefner was a master of seduction. Over time, women who came into the system to become models were introduced to drugs, alcohol, and hard partying. And the women and their bodies became slaves to Hefner and the men who frequented the mansion.

These women came into a system where they were expected to behave in certain ways. They were required to perform repeated actions over and over again. The impact it had on their health (physical, mental, and spiritual) was profound. One model lost all of her teeth because of repeated drug use. Some women simply disappeared, and a few were found dead. Most of the women who came forward after Hefner's death talked openly about the destruction and damage they suffered as a result of their behaviors and the behavior of these oppressive men.

Hefner created an immersive culture of "spiritual formation" in order to modify the behavior of his victims to his wishes. Spiritual formation goes both ways, to either light or darkness.

His immersive culture was so powerful, so formative, that even after the abuse these women suffered, many were still supportive of the Ideas behind Playboy's mission. Meaning that while these women condemned the behavior of the men who exploited them and regretted their own behavior, they still concluded that women posing naked and performing various acts for the camera was empowering and good for women. They still publicly endorsed the Ideas and behaviors that led to their own abuse and exploitation in the first place.

Behavior as a Heartview Indicator

In modern Christianity, we place a high value on behaviors such as prayer, Bible reading, church volunteering, evangelism, and preaching. These are the behaviors of "good Christians." We tend to be quick to praise and esteem church and business leaders who exhibit these behaviors on a regular basis.

However, is that the entire picture? If a pastor is an effective communicator of a religious message, does that automatically mean he is journeying to become more like Jesus? Are so-called spiritual behaviors the primary means by which we come to understand our hearts and the hearts of others?

I'm convinced there is more to the story. Some of the most reprehensible behavior I've ever witnessed came from church leaders who pray frequently, preach with impact, and regularly go on mission trips.

We tend to overemphasize and over-value spiritual behaviors because they give us status in the Christian community. That's why when we evaluate ourselves or others, we should look at various behaviors across all four relationships—with God, others, ourselves, and creation—and not just the public behaviors that score us points with other Christians.

Paul gave Titus some instructions on what he should look for in mature leaders, men and women cultivating Deep Discipleship. The verses below pertain to the office of elder, though I think we would expect and respect these in anyone desiring to become more like our King:

> ...*namely,* if any man is above reproach, the husband of one wife, having children who believe, not accused of dissipation or rebellion. For the overseer must be above reproach as God's steward, not self-willed, not quick-tempered, not addicted to wine, not pugnacious, not fond of sordid gain, but hospitable, loving what is good, sensible, just, devout, self-controlled, holding fast the faithful word which is in accordance with the teaching, so that he will be able both to exhort in sound doctrine and to refute those who contradict.[18]

Let's take careful note of his key phrases: above reproach, faithfully married, solid kids, not rebellious, not self-willed or quick-tempered, not addicted to anything, not greedy. Hospitable, loving what is good, having common sense, just, devout, and self-controlled. And lastly, holding fast to the Word.

In other words, a mature disciple exhibits patterns of behavior that reflect Christ across all four relationships.

Is it possible to pray two hours a day and still lack common sense and self-control? Yes. Is it possible to be an effective evangelist or pastor or elder and be a control freak? Or a narcissist? Yes. Is it possible to exhibit the behaviors of a mature Christian visibly and externally, but have a heart that bends toward darkness? Yes.

When we work with God and trusted friends to evaluate our behaviors as an indicator of our hearts, we do so holistically. We don't just look at our public spiritual behaviors; we look at our repeated actions related to God, to those closest to us, to ourselves, and to our role as stewards of creation.

Why? Because some of us may be masterful at faking behaviors in certain settings.

Conversely, a person of mature character will evidence authenticity and consistency in her behavior in whatever environment she finds herself: at church, at home, with family and friends, or by herself.

As we explore how to use our Eight Indicators to unveil the Ideas in our hearts, we realize how mundane and earthy Heartview is. We dig into our hearts by bringing our indicators to God and a friend with courageous curiosity to explore how these outward signs are pointing back to an inward reality.

Chapter 7 Cumulative Key Takeaways

1. A primary reason for our sense of disconnection and loneliness is the "Great Omission," a struggle to genuinely make people who live and love like Jesus.
2. This journey is often referred to as "spiritual formation," the long-term process of our character being formed more into the character of Jesus. We enter later stages of formation when we explore the Ideas that govern and power us. We call this Deep Discipleship.
3. However, in our current era, Ideas have formed the basis of three systemic and harmful cultural frameworks: the Forgotten Kingdom, the Discipleship Dilemma, and the Formation Gap. We call these the Three Primary Problems.
4. Regarding the second problem, the Discipleship Dilemma, God has ingeniously wired us so that we may uncover and explore the Ideas and desires that sit in the bedrock of our soils. We have eight signposts or indicators that point down to our soils. If we carefully pay attention to these indicators, we may cooperate with God and a trusted friend to dig beneath the surface to transform harmful Ideas into life-giving Ideas. We call this practice "Heartview," and it's the

work of a deep disciple. The first four indicators are our thoughts, emotions, health, and behaviors.

---

1. *The Holy Bible: English Standard Version* (Pr 20:5). (2016). Crossway Bibles.
2. Brian Fisher, "Episode 20: Why Can't We All Just Get Along?" *Soil & Roots*, accessed October 21, 2023, https://www.soilandroots.org/blog/ep-20-why-cant-we-all-just-get-along.
3. René Descartes, "I Think; Therefore I Am," *Dictionary.com*, accessed October 21, 2023, https://www.dictionary.com/browse/i-think-therefore-i-am.
4. Willard, D. (2002). *Renovation of the Heart: Putting on the Character of Christ* (p. 104). NavPress.
5. Proverbs 23:6–8
6. Psalms 139:23–24
7. David Freund, "It's A Paradox #1," *MACNY*, accessed October 21, 2023, https://www.macny.org/its-a-paradox-1/.
8. Thompson, C. (2010). *Anatomy of the Soul: Surprising Connections between Neuroscience and Spiritual Practices that Can Transform Your Life and Relationships* (p. 164). Tyndale Momentum.
9. Dodd, C. (2014). *The Voice of the Heart: A Call to Full Living* (p. xi).
10. Damico, D. (1992). *Faces of Rage* (p. 32). NavPress.
11. Damico, D. *Faces of Rage* (p. 109). NavPress.
12. Dodd, C. *The Voice of the Heart* (p. xiii).
13. Proverbs 3:7–8
14. Proverbs 17:22
15. Proverbs 16:24
16. Proverbs 4:20–22
17. 3 John 2
18. Titus 1:6–9

Eight
The Discipleship Dilemma 2

The heart has its reasons that reason does not know.
—Blaise Pascal[1]

So far, we've touched on four of our Eight Indicators. Our hearts consistently reveal their true Ideas and desires, and God invites us to journey with Him and trusted friends to explore our indicators and what's underneath, which forms the process or habit we call Heartview.

If we pay attention to our thought patterns about God, others, ourselves, and creation, we will gain insight into our heart condition.

Our emotions, though often maligned in our current age, are vital indicators of our Ideas and desires. Exploring why we feel the way we do in various situations often results in wonderful insights about our deep selves.

Likewise, our health (spiritual, physical, emotional) often provides a portal to understanding our hearts. We are integrated beings living in an integrated world. Though external forces often impact our health, it may also be a clear indicator of a wounded spiritual condition.

Our repeated actions, our behaviors, are a goldmine of insight into our soils. By exploring the rhythms of our actions in our four relationships (with God, others, ourselves, and creation and culture), we often glean important visibility into the Ideas that govern us.

Let's finish off our brief explanation of Heartview by introducing the last four indicators: Relationships, Words, Time, and Money.

Relationships

What might we learn about our spirits from how we relate to others?

Modern-day discipleship programs rarely help us understand our own stories. Most programs are focused on Bible passages and studies that provide excellent and stable foundations for growing in our knowledge and experience with Jesus. Though wonderful at helping us grasp and embrace His heart, these programs don't normally guide us into the journey of understanding our own stories and how our stories impact our relationships, not only with Jesus, but with others, ourselves, and creation.

This unwittingly places apprentices of Jesus in a dilemma: in my journey of character formation, am I allowed to explore and understand how my story and history impact all of my relationships now, including my relationship with God?

One of the most powerful uses of exploring our stories as we move ahead in our spiritual formation is in understanding how and why we relate to others and ourselves the way we do. To understand why and how we relate to God, other people, and ourselves the way we do *today*, it's vital we understand our stories all the way back *to our beginning*.

Attachment

Podcaster Adam Young, a Licensed Clinical Social Worker, has frequently commented on a field of study called "Attachment Theory," and he provides a helpful introduction and definition of "attachment."

> God's intention for humanity is not that we would merely live our lives next to each other, but that we would be increasingly known by one another. Attachment is the emotional bond that you develop with a person who will be there for you, and who truly knows you.[2]

As infants, babies, and children, we inherently seek healthy attachments even in our earliest moments.

Young continues, "As a child, your most important attachment was your connection with your primary caregiver. This one relationship shaped your brain more than anything else."[3]

Our primary initial relationships have a profound impact on the rest of our lives—on our emotions and how we express them, on our awareness of ourselves and others, and even on our ability to deal with evil. And, to our purposes, on the cultivation of our Deep Discipleship.

We develop certain styles of how we relate to other people, ourselves, and God based on how our family of origin relates to us.

Six Things Every Child Needs

Young lists six things every child needs from their parent or caregiver:

1. Attunement (a primary caregiver in tune with the child's heart, rather than constantly distracted by their own issues)
2. Responsiveness
3. Engagement (a primary caregiver who desires to truly know the child)
4. The ability to help the child regulate how to handle distress
5. The ability of the caregiver to handle the child's strong emotions (from anger to sadness, from fear to joy)
6. Willingness to repair relational damage (initiating forgiveness and repentance when the caregiver wronged

the child and offering forgiveness in turn when the child misbehaves)

The presence or absence of these six things when we are children results in an *attachment style* that may characterize us for the rest of our lives.

Attachment styles

Those who study attachment typically note four different styles: healthy, avoidant, ambivalent, and disorganized.

If your origin story involves a caregiver who was consistently attuned to you—who willingly focused on your heart, was responsive, was engaged and wanted to truly know you, helped you regulate distress, could handle your strong emotions, and initiated repentance and forgiveness when they wronged you—chances are good that you attach with others and God in a secure manner today. Your attachment style is healthy.

On the other end of the spectrum is the disorganized attachment style, which normally results from a family of substantial harm and abuse. Due to the child experiencing significant trauma in the home, she grows up without any anchor or stability in relationships, and her heart becomes broken. She appears highly dysfunctional and chaotic in relation to other people and God as she matures.

If the child doesn't experience all six things she needs as a child, and absent substantial trauma, she'll probably develop either an avoidant attachment style or an ambivalent attachment style. An avoidant attachment style results when a child grows up with parents who *will not* or *cannot* know the child and aren't attuned to the child, who will unconsciously shut down her heart. To protect herself from future harm, the child's heart simply refuses to engage. An ambivalent attachment style is characterized by insecurity in the child because the caregiver's attention and care are unreliable, unpredictable, and inconsistent. When a child grows up with one of these attachment styles, she isn't conscious of it, and it isn't her fault. Her tender, young heart is forced to adapt to a situation that isn't healthy or secure—even if it looks like it on the outside.

In describing what causes these two styles, avoidant or ambivalent attachment, psychiatrist Curt Thompson writes:

> We can grow up in homes in which the food finds the table, the money finds the college funds, and the family even finds church each Sunday; but somehow our hearts remain undiscovered by the two people we need to know us—our parents.[4]

The Past and the Present

Jesus is securely attached—to His Father, to others, and to Himself. If we wish to become more like Jesus, we also desire to experience secure attachment. It is difficult to take that journey if we don't first evaluate our current style and how it came to be formed.

As an example, consider a child who grows up with parents who are not attuned to her and develops an avoidant attachment style. According to Young, as an adult, she might feel comfortable with distance and separation, focus on the cerebral and analytical (to avoid the pain of missed emotional connections), and insist the past has little effect on her life.

Someone who is avoidantly attached may not have dreams or big ideas. She has some friends, but probably not close ones, as she may not even know what a close friend is supposed to look like. She may be married, but she may also struggle with intimacy and oneness.

And she may have a hard time relating to or hearing from God. After all, if her heart was formed to believe no one wanted to know her when she was a child, why would God want to know her now? She may be a faithful Christian, and she sings the right worship songs and does all the right Bible studies. And yet, her heart remains numb. Inside, she wonders why so many people seem to walk so closely with Jesus, but she can't.

She may assume something is wrong with her. She may not consciously say it, but she thinks of God as somewhat distant. That He may be angry with her or that He disapproves of her. That's not what she reads in her Bible, but it's the Idea her heart embraces. After all, her friends hear from God. He seems to speak to their hearts, encouraging them and whispering words of grace to their spirits. But she doesn't hear from God apart from encouraging verses in the Bible. That only reinforces the Idea that she is somehow faulty.[5]

Or consider someone who is ambivalently attached, who as a child may have experienced some of the six things every child needs from his parents, but the care was erratic, unpredictable, and undependable. In this scenario, the child's heart learns very quickly that mom and dad cannot be relied upon for consistent care. His heart realizes that his parents have other priorities, and they drift in and out of a desire to know their own child.

His heart isn't sure what to do, and this causes anxiety and uncertainty. He may become hyper-attuned to his parents. He responds to his *parents'* emotional needs instead of the other way around.

Young describes how, as an adult, such a person may have difficulty regulating anxiety, feel frantic inside as he struggles to find relief, and be plagued by a deep-seated fear that he is going to be rejected or abandoned, which makes it difficult to trust anyone. He needs constant proof that he is loved, suffers from self-criticism and insecurity, and relies heavily on others to validate his worth through approval and reassurance.[6]

We sometimes think the word "ambivalent" means that someone doesn't care, but it means being caught between two or more strong desires or ideas and not knowing what to do. It's like the proverbial "deer in the headlights."

Those who are ambivalently attached don't know what to expect from relationships and are deeply insecure about them. Constantly searching for affirmation and security, they can be easy marks for narcissists and other predatory personalities outside and inside the church, who will quickly identify them and give them exactly what they desire... until their usefulness has dried up.

A person with ambivalent attachment is unsure about his earthly relationships, but may also be insecure and anxious about his relationship with God. Does God love him based on how he performs—based on how many Christian things he does? This isn't what he reads in Scripture, but his heart struggles to relate to God as a loving Father, as a being who wants to be known and wants an intimate, secure relationship with us. His bedrock Ideas are different from his theological beliefs.

How does an ambivalently attached person know that God really accepts him and truly wants to know him? After all, he isn't sure if anyone wants to truly know him. When things go badly, is God punishing him? When things go well, is there another shoe that God is waiting to drop? He struggles to rest in the presence of God because his heart hasn't been formed to rest at all.

The formation of a certain attachment style in the human heart is not the person's fault. It's unconscious and a result of growing up in a family of origin that may have its own deep challenges. But as we mature, we can identify the signs of each, and when it comes to disorganized, ambivalent, or avoidant attachment styles, we can recognize that hurting people hurt people. People often end up treating people like they have been treated—even unconsciously.

As we embrace Deep Discipleship, the relationships we form—and our earliest stories, which help define them—can be a powerful indicator of our hearts.

Words

Words may well be the least reliable of our indicators.

It's not that words can't be an effective way of uncovering the Ideas and desires in our hearts. But talk really can be cheap, and we tend to be fabulous, sophisticated liars—to ourselves and others.

However, since we spend so much time talking and using our words, let's briefly explore how we might use them to journey into Deep Discipleship.

Jesus had a lot to say about words. In Matthew 12, He said:

> Either make the tree good and its fruit good, or make the tree bad and its fruit bad; for the tree is known by its fruit. You brood of vipers, how can you, being evil, speak what is good? For the mouth speaks out of that which fills the heart. The good man brings out of his good treasure what is good; and the evil man brings out of his evil treasure what is evil. But I tell you that every careless word that people speak, they shall give an accounting for it in the day of judgment. For by your words you will be justified, and by your words you will be condemned.[7]

All Eight Indicators are found in Scripture, but perhaps not quite as blatantly as "words," as we note in verse 34: "for the mouth speaks out of that which fills the heart."

Volume of Words

Let's explore how our volume of words may be an indicator of Ideas and desires in our hearts.

Chances are you have some friends or family members who use lots of words. While it seems to be true that men, overall, tend to use fewer words than women, being loquacious isn't always gender specific.

And certainly, folks with extroverted, excitable characteristics can be talkative. Others are verbal processors; they think out loud. They use lots of words because that's how they sort out information so they may make good conclusions and decisions.

However, there's a difference between someone who may simply like to talk a lot and someone who dominates a conversation. They may be great storytellers and have insightful comments, though they come across as domineering, impolite, maybe a touch arrogant, and selfish. At some point, we end up concluding a hyper-talkative person really doesn't care about anyone else's story or opinion. They're too busy sharing their own.

This use of words is an indicator of certain desires and Ideas in their hearts. Whether they're attempting to prove themselves, gain status, intimidate others, or prevent someone else from asking a question they may not know the answer to, a hyper-talkative person is generally someone who has control issues, insecurities, or a deep need for attention.

The Gospels only provide insight into a fraction of Jesus's social interactions while He was on the planet, but it's clear that Jesus measured His words thoughtfully and was deeply, intentionally engaged with people. He listened very carefully. He was intuitive, challenging, and, at times, uncomfortable in the way he probed people's hearts.

His conversation with the Syrophoenician woman in Matthew 15 is one of my all-time favorite stories. Jesus appears to ignore this Gentile woman who is begging Him to heal her demon-possessed little daughter. The disciples get annoyed, and Jesus further dismisses the woman by saying that He came for the lost sheep of Israel. In other words, He didn't come for Gentiles—for her.

She persists, and now it seems Jesus insults her. He tells her it isn't good to give children's bread to the dogs! But she takes His comment and turns it around, reminding Jesus that even the dogs can eat the crumbs that fall off the table. She recognizes Jesus had come initially for the nation of Israel and accepts her position as a Gentile, and yet she still begs Him to heal her daughter.

Jesus has been testing her, inviting her into a deeper engagement with Him, and she accepts His invitation. He recognizes and compliments her faith, and He heals her daughter.

It's a striking exchange and shows just how intentional, attuned, and even curious Jesus is. First, He appears to ignore her, then He makes it clear she isn't in His target audience, and then He reminds her of how Jewish society viewed her (not very favorably)—all in a gentle process of uncovering her heart and the depth of her faith. And most likely gives His disciples another much-needed lesson in the process.

This type of social interaction requires a heart that is purposefully bent toward learning about other people. About wanting to know them —not just the surface stuff we talk about at church, but the actual condition of our hearts. And we simply can't do that if we're the only ones talking.

Proverbs is filled with instructions about our speech, but one of my favorites is in Chapter 10:

> When there are many words, transgression is unavoidable, but he who restrains his lips is wise.[8]

Mark Twain said, "The right word may be effective, but no word was ever as effective as a rightly timed pause."[9]

Or as French philosopher Voltaire put it, "The secret of being boring is to say everything."[10]

Instinctual Words

A second example of how to explore our words as indicators of what's going on in our hearts is to pay attention to what we say when we don't have time to prepare. This is what we say off the cuff, when we're caught off guard or emotional, or when we quickly respond to something without thinking about it.

We tend to be sophisticated liars when we have time to prepare for what to say. This is why it's fascinating to explore the words we say when we don't have that time. We might call these our *instinctual words*.

In evaluating our instinctual words, we may discover our heart bends toward the kingdom of light. When someone is hurting, we instinctually speak words of grace and compassion without thinking about it. When someone cuts us off in traffic, our immediate non-thinking response is to ignore their mistake and go about our day. Or perhaps we note they cut us off in traffic with some frustration, which we certainly have the right to do, but our words don't include any colorful descriptions of the other driver, if you know what I mean. And I think you know what I mean.

When a family member disrespects us, our non-thinking response may include pointing out their error, but in a way that promotes mutual respect. When we see an injustice, our instinct is to call it out in clear terms while still recognizing that every human being bears the image of God.

Sometimes, though, our instinctual words uncover less desirable things about our hearts. A sharp word to a spouse. An unthinking, callous word to our children. Frustration expressed with someone in a way that doesn't honor them.

There are moments for appropriately challenging, provocative, or even harsh words. Jesus used some very harsh language and even name-calling when dealing with certain types of people, but His heart was always oriented toward love. Ours are not always oriented in that direction.

We may take an inventory of the words we say instinctually—the things we say without thinking. And, if we really want to understand our hearts, we may ask those close to us about our instinctual words. Chances are we've forgotten some of the things we said—and chances are those closest to us haven't.

The Words We Don't Speak

Lastly, we learn about our own hearts and those around us by paying attention to what we don't say and to the words we hold back.

Some people avoid engaging in conversation about areas that prick their hearts. I've had friends throughout my life who communicate entirely above the surface. They'll talk about work, sports, theology, church, and maybe even family. But anytime they're invited to dig under the surface—to talk about desires, Ideas, wounds, stories—they close up.

Again, what the Bible tells us about Jesus's social interactions shows a man who continually cut through the small talk and invited people to explore the depths of their hearts. He was constantly healing, constantly restoring, constantly challenging, constantly provoking His disciples and His followers to crawl through the legalism, the power structures, the social mores, the religiosity, and the unconscious Ideas in the culture of His time, and to meet Him in the realm of our Ideas and desires.

If we carefully pay attention to how much we say, what we say when we aren't thinking, and what we intentionally avoid saying, we get a peek at the recesses of our hearts.

Time

Benjamin Franklin famously said, "...Time is money."[11] The hedonist Oscar Wilde didn't agree; he said, "Time is a waste of money."[12]

And President Kennedy said, "We must use time as a tool, not as a couch."[13]

But John Wanamaker noted, "People who cannot find time for recreation are obliged sooner or later to find time for illness."[14]

Louis E. Boone wrote, "I am definitely going to take a course on time management... just as soon as I can work it into my schedule."[15]

While Douglas Adams joked, "I love deadlines. I like the whooshing sound they make as they fly by."[16]

Time, our seventh Heartview Indicator, is perhaps the most complex, curious, and mysterious of our Eight Indicators.

We have at least some control over our thoughts, emotions, and behaviors. We can take charge of our health to varying degrees. We choose to whom we relate, and we at least try to control our words. And we have tremendous flexibility in how we manage our money.

But time is unique. It's fixed and entirely outside of our control. We can't choose to stop the clock. We're all caught in a steady march of time—and we are entirely incapable of leaving the parade.

It's both wonderful and a little scary. There is comfort in knowing a minute is 60 seconds, and it will continue to be 60 seconds until time ends. There is security in knowing that today is 24 hours. Tomorrow will also be 24 hours. Next Thursday will consist of 24 hours. Yet, no matter what we do, we live in a fixed reality of time that we can't influence, and we don't even know how much of it we really have.

A simple way of exploring time as an indicator of the desires and Ideas in our hearts is to remind ourselves of what our mothers told us: we always make time to do the things we really want to do. So, how we steward our time shows us what or whom we love.

A basic but helpful exercise in determining our true Ideas and desires is to inventory our time for a few weeks. We may be shocked at how many minutes or hours we actually spend working, doom scrolling on our phones, engaged with our families, deepening our marriages, or binge-watching TV simply by keeping an honest log of our time.

You may have had a youth group leader or pastor teach you that if you want to grow to be like Jesus, you need to spend time with Jesus. Makes sense. There are plenty of guilt-inducing studies that show how much time we spend on spiritual or religious activities. *Christianity Today* reports the average American spends nine minutes per day on spiritual habits.[17]

A bit more optimistically, the website Patheos calculated that the average practicing Christian spends around four hours a week on religious activities.[18] That's a more positive average of around 35 minutes per day. That sounds about right if we attend church for 90 minutes per week, engage in a Bible study on a weekday or attend a small group, and have daily devotions and prayer time.

However, as Bob Robinson points out, for the Christian, there is no secular or sacred.[19] There's only sacred. How do we measure "religious" or "spiritual" time? Is eating a meal somehow less sacred than our prayer time if all time belongs to God? Is resting or enjoying a hobby somehow less spiritual than singing hymns and worship songs at church? Many of us would instinctively feel, in our hearts, that certain activities are more or less religious or spiritual. But if our entire lives are to be an expression of worship—of love and devotion—to God, why would we segment our time into spiritual and non-spiritual?

I love my wife. I also like her. We intentionally spend a fair amount of time together, not because it's a ritual or a chore, but because we genuinely like each other's company and we *enjoy* growing closer together.

The Westminster Shorter Catechism says that the chief end of man is to glorify God and *enjoy Him forever*.[20] Can we enjoy God by eating a meal or watching a ballgame? Sure. Those are good gifts from God.

Still, if we spend 30 hours a week watching sports but only two minutes a day reading our Bible and praying, we probably shouldn't wonder why we aren't getting to know Jesus better. This is just common sense. Time is a requirement for any relationship. And if you love someone, you want to spend time with them. Not because you *have* to, but because it's a joy to be with them.

We can learn a lot about what we love and about the Ideas that drive us by inventorying our time. As a short example, people who work consistently long hours out of choice (not requirement) desire things that work gives them, and these desires are tied to their Ideas, typically to their Ideas of identity and value. They derive their identity and value from work, so the indicator of their time points to these Ideas in their hearts.

Money

Money has been at the center of debate, discussion, romance, marriage, divorce, good health, bad health, prosperity, poverty, peace, war, virtue, and vice since the beginning of time. Is there anything so fundamental... and so controversial... to human life and existence as money?

The Bible has an abundance to say about money. There are some 500 Bible verses that mention prayer. And there are over 2,000 verses that refer to money.

Money, as our last Heartview Indicator, provides perhaps the fastest and most accurate look into our hearts.

Early in my career, I worked in the financial services industry and became what's known as a Certified Financial Planner®. A CFP® serves families on all sorts of financial issues, such as investments, insurance, estate planning, and taxation.

When I worked as an executive in the investment world, I also became certified in a course on biblical stewardship, or how to use money according to the principles found in Scripture. I would hold workshops on how to build a family budget, and I worked with families to help them craft financial plans for their future.

I was pretty young in my career when I conducted budgeting workshops, though I was certain my education and insight would lead family after family to financial freedom through my wisdom and experience crafting God-honoring plans.

But about a year or two into teaching biblical financial principles, I came to a humbling realization: the majority of people who took my classes either never used the budget they had just successfully built, or they tried it for a month or two and then quit. I came away from the experience wondering if I was just exemplifying the old adage, "You can lead a horse to water, but you can't make him drink."

Though some people do have a balanced and wise approach to money, I realized I could categorize most people into two basic groups. I called them "wardens" and "wingers."

Wardens

A warden is someone who clings tightly to money. Money is their prisoner. They love to get it and save it, though they're reluctant to spend it. They live in fear of losing their money, so they watch it closely, invest it wisely but conservatively, and may experience substantial anxiety when the market doesn't go their way or when they incur a large, unexpected expense.

The amount of money a warden makes isn't really the issue; it's the way they treat the money they make.

Wardens can be generous, but they're typically very concerned with the ROI of their charitable giving and tend to find excuses not to give. They resonate with Bible verses about thriftiness and diversification, such as Ecclesiastes 11:2, which says, "Divide your portion to seven, or even to eight, for you do not know what misfortune may occur on the earth."[21] They can be mistrustful of friends and relatives who may appear to be trying to take advantage of the warden.

Wardens not only treat money as their prisoner—they can create a prison for themselves. They become a prisoner of their money.

Wingers

And then there are the wingers. They "wing it." If they want something, they buy it. If they can't afford it, they buy it anyway. They wield silver crosses and cloves of garlic if you mention the word "budget," and they generally live paycheck to paycheck, though this normally doesn't have to do with the amount of money they make.

Wingers can be very generous, even to a fault. They tend to heavily spiritualize their giving. God "tells them to give sacrificially," even if they're swamped in credit card debt. They believe in living by faith, which to a winger means they don't or can't control their spending and expect God to reward them with provision anyhow because they are so faithful. When they overspend or overgive and survive the next month, they credit God for honoring their faithfulness.

They tend to give as freely as they spend, without much responsibility or thought. A winger steers clear of Bible verses about discipline, delayed gratification, and stewardship, instead focusing on verses about God's grace, His overflowing abundance, and His passionate love for us.

On the extreme ends of these two categories of people, we find some deeply harmful dysfunction. A warden can become a hoarder, plagued by anxiety, fear, and suspicion. A winger can turn into a gambler, an irresponsible entrepreneur, or someone who exhibits very high-risk behaviors.

Much of the time, wardens and wingers look like everyday good Christians, even though deep down in their hearts, they're struggling with common dark Ideas and desires.

Not everyone is a full-blown warden or winger, of course, but most of us tend in one direction or the other. If you're not sure about yourself, just ask your spouse or a close friend! There's a high probability they will quickly tell you whether you treat money like your prisoner or your liberator.

Money as a Heartview Indicator

Money presents an incredible incentive for us to embrace Ideas of darkness because of the power and security it represents.

Ironically, the warden and the winger both struggle with the same dark Ideas, even though the ways they treat money end up looking different.

The Bible says the love of money is the root of all evil. It's not wrong to have a lot of money, and lots of Americans have lots of money. As we're exploring with Heartview, our concern is not with the outward indicator, but with the condition of our hearts.

To the warden, money represents control, security, and power. And, like most people, the warden desires those things. Why do wardens desire control, security, and power? Because those things have been taken from them at some point in their lives.

It's not necessarily that *money* has been stolen from them, but that other things have been stolen—such as their value, their purpose, and their identity. In many cases, their deepest desire... to be known, to be seen, to be wanted by someone... went unfulfilled. Or they were abandoned or betrayed at some point.

Someone who longs to be known and is instead rejected becomes understandably angry. That doesn't mean they necessarily rant and rave around the house; it means they yearn for control. Their heart doesn't want to continue hurting, so to protect itself, it seeks things it can control. A warden unconsciously assumes that by controlling something—anything—she can keep herself from harm.

Controlling behavior is almost always associated with anger and rage, and it shows up in our financial habits all the time. Why?

Because money is an incredibly accessible, easy, powerful thing to control. Many people have a deeply embedded Idea of what money represents, especially in Christian communities. Money supposedly means God has blessed you. If you're financially successful, people look up to you. They give you respect and honor. If you're wealthy, you're invited to corporate boards and church governing bodies. You are asked to speak and to give advice. It's assumed you must be wise since you are adept at business and have accumulated money.

Instead of the heart of the warden seeking its acceptance and security in God, it finds its desires met in money. A warden often unconsciously seeks the power and control that money supposedly represents because she struggles to trust God fully.

Why? Because her heart was powerfully formed around the Idea that God couldn't be trusted. She is not alone in her struggle. We need only to return to Genesis 3 to understand why.

A warden is wounded. Her mind and mouth will say all the accepted Christian things, but her distrust of God and her tentativeness in giving up control to Him come out in the way she views and handles money. Because her heart is scared to give itself fully to God, she instead takes control so that she feels safe, in control, and secure.

The warden tends to think the winger is nuts, at least after they've gotten to know each other.

When I've observed a warden marry a winger, the initial story goes like this. The winger comes across as carefree, fun, romantic, and adventurous. To the warden, this is a breath of fresh air. The winger seems so secure. The warden longs for the freedom and relaxation the winger seems to enjoy all the time. The winger is attracted to the warden because of the responsibility and structure they represent.

It's romantic until they get married. The warden quickly concludes that the winger is not carefree and secure; he is irresponsible and theatrical. The winger isn't free from anxiety. He is just deflecting his anxiety and refusing to deal with it.

The financial prison the warden constructs becomes real to the winger very quickly. Why can't we just enjoy life? Money is a gift from God, so let's enjoy His blessings! The winger feels constricted, ignored, and hemmed in. What he thought was security was really just a set of walls around his carefree personality.

The winger, though, is also wounded. But instead of seeking to control money and use it as a security blanket, the winger simply ignores money problems and acts as if it will all work out. Where the warden is a professional at delayed gratification, the winger gratifies himself immediately because (and here's the point) he fully believes he deserves it.

He deserves what was stolen from him. He has the same wounds as the warden: a loss of identity, value, power, purpose, or love. His heart desires to be known as well, and that desire was corrupted or abandoned somewhere in his story. And his heart is understandably angry. You rarely see the anger in the speech or emotions of a winger, but it visibly appears in the way he treats money.

He pays the restaurant bill even when he can't afford it. He wants to be seen as generous. If he wants a new toy, he buys it. It's not really about the toy; it's about the feeling it brings. He's easily frustrated when his friends have things he can't have, so he buys them because, well, he deserves it. He's had a tough day, or a tough month, or a tough life.

He'll often use his wife or his kids as justification for his spending. He believes his kids deserve the same things other kids have. So, he spends the money and will figure out how to pay for everything down the road.

A winger is also angry—perhaps even enraged—and generally doesn't know it. He uses money to soothe his anger by trying to fulfill unmet or broken deep desires.

Wardens and wingers seem like opposites, but they're not. They share the same wounds and the same consequences. They both use money to attempt to fulfill their bedrock desires and to soothe their pain. One does it by controlling money, and the other does it by letting the money control them.

And both of their hearts struggle to trust God because their hearts believe God has let them down, that He can't be trusted.

So, if we discover through our talks with God and trusted friends that we are wardens or wingers more often than not, what do we do?

As with any Heartview Indicator, finding healing and becoming more like Christ requires understanding our story. If our deepest desire is to be known (to be accepted and loved and to know that someone will be there for us), at what point in our story was that desire broken, abandoned, or damaged by someone who was supposed to be there for us?

Wardens and wingers can experience freedom if they're courageously curious about their stories.

Wardens remain responsible, savvy investors and stewards of their money, though they don't depend on their money to soothe their anger and their pain. Money is their tool, not their prisoner.

Wingers adapt to budgets, move toward responsible money management, and experience the joy of doing it! Not because of a course or a training program, but because of a healed heart. Money is their tool, not their liberator.

Uncover. Determine. Immerse.

As we close our brief look at the process of Heartview as a means of helping to solve the Discipleship Dilemma, you may be struck by how earthy, how commonsensical, and how mundane it is.

You may be asking, "Can we understand our heart condition better by looking at our money habits than by evaluating how often we go to church?" On the whole, yes.

"How I speak to myself, my spouse, and my kids is a better indicator of my Deep Discipleship than how many Bible verses I've memorized?" On the whole, yes.

"Do most people live their lives without ever exploring their indicators and so miss out on the depth and breadth of their formative journey to become more like Jesus?" For the most part, yes.

So why don't more people engage in the practice of Heartview with God and trusted friends in order to deepen their journey?

There are various reasons. Many of us are born into Ideas in the Air that work against our formation. We have certain assumptions about our comfort, about suffering, and about prosperity that deter us from Heartview and the indicators.

Perhaps an undiagnosed health condition is a sign of a deeper spiritual condition. However, we assume medication is the only approach toward relief, and we expect instant results.

Perhaps our constant anxiety is a sign of corrupted Ideas in our hearts, though we've been repeatedly taught to "be anxious for nothing," so to seek a deeper meaning for our anxiety in the church may be mistaken for weak faith.

Perhaps we have harmful patterns of behavior toward our spouse and children, but we insist on blaming it on surface issues such as work or money problems. Meanwhile, the corrupted Ideas and desires in our soils remain unhealed.

Engaging in Heartview requires a courageous curiosity and the help of God and trusted friends.

However, if we faithfully deepen our relationship with Jesus while deepening our understanding of our own hearts, we are well on our way to experiencing the abundant life, the abiding life, the life without lack that the Bible promises.

Our journey into Deep Discipleship so far has uncovered some surprises. In our era, we are born into an Idea ecosystem hallmarked by Three Primary Problems. Our first problem is the West has forgotten the kingdom. Yet, if our spiritual journey to become more like our King means embracing not only His characteristics but also His mission, embracing His kingdom purpose is central to our discipleship. We also face a Discipleship Dilemma, in that becoming more like Him involves us better understanding Him and His story and ourselves and our stories. Exploring our own hearts and stories is not a Western facet of discipleship, yet God invites us to do just that. A simple way to get started is to sit with God and a trusted friend and practice evaluating our Eight Indicators using Heartview.

The third Primary Problem attaches itself to the first two. The last step of Heartview is "Immerse," or locating and diving into communities specifically designed to form and transform our Ideas. Do these types of communities still exist today? If so, am I already a part of one? If not, how can I find one? Let's move ahead and explore the Formation Gap.

Chapter 8 Cumulative Key Takeaways

1. A primary reason for our sense of disconnection and loneliness is the "Great Omission," a struggle to genuinely make people who live and love like Jesus. We sense there is more to the Christian life, but we're not sure what it is or how to experience it.
2. This sense of "there being more" or "disconnection" is resolved through the journey of genuine discipleship, often

referred to as "spiritual formation." We experience the promises of the Christian life by becoming more like Jesus.

3. We are governed and powered by Ideas (embedded, typically unconscious, experienced assumptions about reality). To explore these Ideas is to engage in Deep Discipleship, the journey into the latter stages of our spiritual formation.
4. However, in our current era, Ideas have formed the basis of three systemic and harmful cultural frameworks: the Forgotten Kingdom, the Discipleship Dilemma, and the Formation Gap.
5. We help resolve the second problem, the Discipleship Dilemma, by courageously exploring our own hearts with God and a trusted friend. We call this practice "Heartview," and it's the work of a deep disciple. Every human being reveals their heart through Eight Indicators. The indicators are our thoughts, emotions, health, behaviors, relationships, words, and how we steward our time and money.

---

1. Matt D'Antuono, "The Heart Has Its Reasons That Reason Does Not Know: The Reason of the Heart is Instinctive Recognition of Truth, Goodness and Beauty," *National Catholic Register*, accessed October 21, 2023, https://www.ncregister.com/blog/the-heart-has-its-reasons-that-reason-does-not-know.
2. Adam Young, "Attachment: What It Is and Why It Matters," *Adam Young Counseling*, accessed October 21, 2023, https://adamyoungcounseling.com/free-documents/.
3. Ibid.
4. Young, A. (Creator). (2018, April 16). "Why Your Family of Origin Impacts Your Life More Than Anything Else" [Audio podcast episode]. *The Place We Find Ourselves.* https://theplacewefindourselves.libsyn.com/2-why-your-family-of-origin-impacts-your-life-more-than-anything-else
5. Adam Young, "Attachment: What it is and Why It Matters," https://adamyoungcounseling.com/free-documents/.
6. Ibid.
7. Matthew 12:33–37
8. Proverbs 10:19

9. *The Writings of Mark Twain [pseud.]: Mark Twain's speeches* (ed. 1929). Stormfield Edition. Harper, 1929.
10. Voltaire, "Quotes by Voltaire," Goodreads.com, accessed November 24, 2023, https://www.goodreads.com/quotes/2565-the-secret-of-being-a-bore-is-to-tell-everything.
11. Benjamin Franklin, "'Advice to a Young Tradesman' (1748)," *UTexas*, accessed October 30, 2023, https://minio.la.utexas.edu/webeditor-files/coretexts/pdf/174820franklin20advice.pdf.
12. Admin, "These Oscar Wilde Quotes Will Blow You Away," *The Genuine Irish Old Moore's Almanac,* accessed October 30, 2023, https://oldmooresalmanac.com/oscar-wilde-quotes/.
13. John F. Kennedy, "John F. Kennedy Quotations," *John F. Kennedy: Presidential Library and Museum,* accessed October 30, 2023, https://www.jfklibrary.org/learn/about-jfk/life-of-john-f-kennedy/john-f-kennedy-quotations#:~:text=%22We%20-must%20use%20time%20as,moment%20but%20for%20our%20time.
14. John Wanamaker, "More Quotes by John Wanamaker," *ForbesQuotes: Thoughts On The Business Of Life,* accessed October 30, 2023, https://www.forbes.com/quotes/author/john-wanamaker/.
15. Larry Hart, "No Time? No Excuse! Read this to Eliminate Distractions and Maximize Time," *CEOTribe: Coaching Executives Online,* accessed October 30, 2023, https://ceotribe.com/blog/no-time-no-excuse-read-eliminate-distractions-maximise-time/.
16. Brian Rowe, "5 Quotes by Douglas Adams to Make You a Better Writer," *Medium,* accessed October 30, 2023, https://writingcooperative.com/5-quotes-by-douglas-adams-to-make-you-a-better-writer-5dc027defd7a.
17. "Average Time Americans Spend in Religious or Spiritual Activities," *ChristianityToday,* accessed October 30, 2023, https://www.preachingtoday.com/illustrations/2010/september/5090610.html.
18. Bob Robinson, "168 Hours: How Much of it Do You Devote to God?", *Patheos,* accessed October 30, 2023, https://www.patheos.com/blogs/reintegrate/2021/04/30/168-hours-how-much-of-it-do-you-devote-to-god/.
19. Bob Robinson, "Dualistic Christianity and the Church," *Patheos,* accessed October 30, 2023, https://www.patheos.com/blogs/reintegrate/2012/08/27/dualistic-christianity/.
20. "The Westminster Shorter Catechism," *The Presbytery of the United States: Free Church of Scotland (Continuing),* accessed October 30, 2023, https://www.westminsterconfession.org/resources/confessional-standards/the-westminster-shorter-catechism/.
21. Ecclesiastes 11:2

Nine
The Formation Gap

> In the house of God there are many mansions. There is a place for everyone—a unique, special place. Once we deeply trust that we ourselves are precious in God's eyes, we are able to recognize the preciousness of others and their unique places in God's heart.
>
> —Henri Nouwen[1]

We now come to the third and final problem facing the West today—the Formation Gap. It is, in many ways, a downstream effect of the first two problems.

If we have forgotten the kingdom, we fail to understand the full mission, nature, and character of our King.

That presents a Discipleship Dilemma because the definition of a disciple is an apprentice of Jesus for the purpose of becoming more like Him. If we don't understand Him as the current and reigning King, we will miss the mark of our formation. Our dilemma is intensified by the fact that being formed more like Him requires us to know our own hearts well.

A person journeying into Deep Discipleship consistently uncovers their own heart and the hearts of those around them by exploring our Eight Indicators through the practice of Heartview. If we aren't attuned to our own hearts and those around us, we will find our journey into Deep Discipleship stunted.

Being formed into Jesus is a journey best taken with others. To that end, many modern Christians do not have access to communities specifically designed to form us. And the consequences have been severe.

The Gap

If Western Christians have access to more teaching than any generation in history, would we not expect a majority of Christians to love, think, act, and relate like Jesus? Then why is the divorce rate inside the Christian church so high? Why is the abortion rate inside the church so high? Why is pornography usage among church members and leaders so high? Why does the average American Christian tithe just 2.5 percent (it was 3.3 percent during the Great Depression)?[2] Why are we fed a constant stream of news stories highlighting Christian leaders who have morally fallen?

Some might argue that the cause of the Western church's struggle to form mature disciples is a lack of biblical orthodoxy.

That's a difficult argument to defend in light of the #MeToo movement and repeated stories of pastors, denominational leaders, apologists, and church administrators admitting to sexual harassment or admitting to covering it up. Some of these stories come from liberal denominations, but many come from denominations and conventions that are typically categorized as holding to traditional biblical truth. Some of the voices we've relied on to preach biblical orthodoxy are the ones embracing the Ideas of darkness they are preaching against.

Another popular response to this apparent paradox of ubiquitous Christian instruction combined with a lack of Deep Discipleship is, "Well, we are all sinners."

Though certainly true, this explanation falls short of the expectation of biblical discipleship.

If we are intentionally growing to become more like Jesus, we should expect to love more deeply, develop extraordinary compassion for ourselves and others, and sin less. I'm not advocating for perfectionism, but certainly, we should expect to sin less five years from now than we do today. We should expect our habitual favorite sins to fade. Our deepest desires should align more and more with the desires of our King and less and less with our flesh. This expectation is woven throughout Scripture, and the theological term to describe it is sanctification.

Our struggles to become deep disciples and reform and help a weakening church are not due to a lack of biblical teaching or a lack of orthodoxy. Our struggles are due to the fact that we live in a Formation Gap. To understand this, let's take a brief look at how human hearts are formed.

The Five Key Elements of Spiritual Formation

Many of our core Ideas are developed when we are very young. As is often repeated, the most formative years of our lives are our earliest ones, from pre-birth to perhaps eight or ten years of age.

When considering a small child, what environmental elements are in place that form her into a mature adult? What elements form her heart, her spirit, and her character?

Though our post-Enlightenment culture tends to assume we are formed primarily through information, is this true for a baby or a young toddler? Is her character only formed by her parents giving her verbal or written instruction?

That's doubtful. A young boy or girl's heart is primarily formed by a wonderful mixture of five critical elements: time, habit, intimacy, community, and instruction.

Time: How much time does a baby or toddler spend with her primary caregivers? In a healthy situation, she spends enormous amounts of time with them. In her earliest years, a caregiver is with her virtually every waking moment and nearby even when she is sleeping.

Habit: What habits are her caregivers instilling in her, even at a very young age? What rituals, traditions, or repetitive behaviors are part of her formation? Sleeping, eating, playing, being held, just gazing into the eyes of her mother or father. In healthy situations, babies and toddlers are introduced to many life-giving habits.

Intimacy: This includes things such as touch, vocal tone, emotional closeness, and presence. A baby in a loving home constantly and willingly experiences intimacy: physical, emotional, and spiritual intimacy. Her caregivers are constantly giving themselves to the child. They share themselves with their child.

Community: In a stable setting, a child is introduced to consistent relationships with secure, predictable people. This certainly includes her caregivers and her siblings, though also perhaps extended family or close friends and playmates. From her earliest moments, the child is in a community of other people who can be relied upon to be there.

Instruction: A baby starts receiving instruction from her parents after just a few short months of life outside the womb. She is quickly taught what to touch and not to touch, what to eat and not to put in her mouth. Her caregivers, through a variety of means, teach her how to navigate the world, relationships, and the basic tasks of everyday life.

Time, habit, intimacy, community, instruction. These are the five basic elements of a child's character formation. Her underlying Ideas about herself and her world are not solely or even primarily formed through instruction. They are formed through relationships and experience.

The Five Key Elements in Adults

So, how does our ongoing heart formation occur as we age? If time, habit, intimacy, community, and instruction are the basis for a child's character/spiritual formation, what are the basic elements for our spiritual formation as adults? Or, stated differently, what are the necessary components of Deep Discipleship?

Not surprisingly, they are time, habit, intimacy, community, and instruction, the exact same five elements.

There is some irony here in that we tend to be very comfortable with five-element formative communities, except when it comes to our discipleship.

We've already explored early childhood, which is an intensive, five-element immersive experience.

We expect the military to embody all five elements. In order to form a civilian into a soldier, we assume and expect the military to invest time, considerable habits, an immersive community, trust and transparency, and appropriate instruction in order to properly form their enlistees.

Most college experiences embrace all five elements. Students live with each other, they are trained in numerous study and life habits, and they form a myriad of communities around interests and subjects. It's generally a time of cultivating deep and trusted friendships, and instruction abounds, both in and out of the classroom.

Even our cultural assumptions about marriage embrace all five elements. Husband and wife give up time with other people and pursuits to come together as one. A plethora of habits undergoes formation and reformation as the new family comes together. A healthy marriage will be a community of two, though it will also find a wider identity in other related groups. Intimacy is, obviously, a crucial component of any healthy marriage, and instruction (the exchange of information) is perpetual as husband and wife grow in their immersive relationship.

However, drastic changes in both the church and culture over the last few hundred years have eroded most of the elements our ancestors took for granted.

Jesus and the Five Elements

Let's take a look at how Jesus modeled discipleship and the five elements.

Time: How much time did Jesus spend with His close friends? He lived with them. For three years, they ate, slept, talked, and traveled together. They appear to have been in each other's presence much of the time.

Even after Pentecost, as disciples began to multiply, there is a strong sense that Christians lived, ate, and worked with each other. Acts 2 talks about the earliest Christians devoting themselves to teaching, fellowship, breaking of bread, and prayer. They learned together, ate together, prayed together, and lived together.

On their first few journeys, the traveling missionaries would typically spend months, if not years, in one location, living with their apprentices and students. Eating, working, talking, serving—just doing life together.

Habit: What habits did Jesus model for His friends and disciples? Certainly, teaching and prayer. Rest. Eating. It's striking just how often meals come up in the Bible.

However, Jesus modeled some other habits we don't always pick up on.

Based on what we read, Jesus didn't engage in a lot of small talk or patronizing questions. Instead, He was incredibly quick at getting to the heart of the person with whom He was interacting. The woman at the well. The rich young ruler. The Pharisees. Nicodemus. Peter.

Jesus was deeply, irresistibly concerned with the hearts of those around him. He typically steered the conversations to the condition of people's hearts. He uncovered their pride, their arrogance, their legalism. He gently unveiled their brokenness, their wounds, their fractures.

Though He dealt with the arrogant differently than the humble, He intentionally invited them all to peer under the surface. He invited them to explore their roots and soil, even when it was painful.

This was one of His habits: inviting those around Him to drop their pretense and to experience Jesus as the fulfillment of their heart's true desires. This is evident in both His public preaching and His personal interactions.

Yet another of Jesus's habits was restoration. Jesus was constantly healing physically, but also spiritually and culturally. When He healed the woman who had been bleeding for many years, He didn't just heal her body. She was no longer ceremonially unclean. Jesus restored her to her community.

Jesus embraced children at a time when children were often considered throwaways and afterthoughts. But He hugged them and blessed them. He restored them to their proper place as image-bearers of their Creator.

He scandalously engaged a Samaritan woman and restored her. He challenged her use of men to satisfy the desires of her heart and instead presented Himself as her only source of true fulfillment.

Jesus restored, not only to physical health, but to restoration in all four of the relationships we've discussed: God, self, others, and creation and culture. That was one of His primary habits.

Intimacy: Did Jesus model intimacy with His disciples?

Jesus was careful to whom He gave His heart. He didn't treat everyone the same. He was most vulnerable with His inner circle of three friends, though He gave Himself freely to the 12 apostles. He shared His heart, His plans, His future, and His pain.

Though they fell asleep on Him, a few of His disciples witnessed His extraordinary emotional suffering before the cross. His three closest friends saw His transfiguration. Within His tight community, He was surprisingly vulnerable, transparent, and open-hearted.

Community: As mentioned, the 12 disciples and the other women and men who traveled with Him were Jesus's closest community. They did life together. Discipleship happens relationally in a committed group of friends. After Pentecost, we see a similar pattern of churches springing up in tight-knit communities of families and close friends.

Author Robert Coleman remarked, "Reading the Acts, one gets the impression that the Christians just enjoyed doing things together. In these casual relationships, probably more than in their gathered meetings, they learned what it meant to follow Christ in the daily routine of life."[3]

Instruction: This is what we typically think of as discipleship, and Jesus certainly instructed. He instructed the masses differently than His 12 friends. His instructions turned the world upside down. Through His instruction, His example, and His behavior, Jesus confronted and challenged the governing Ideas of His day.

> Changing those governing ideas is one of the most difficult and painful things in life... Jesus confronted and undermined an idea system and its culture, which in turn killed him. He proved himself greater than any idea system or culture, and he lives on. He is continuing the process of a worldwide idea shift that is crucial to *his* perpetual revolution, in which we each are assigned a part.[4]

The Five Elements Today

We've explored how our core Ideas are formed both as children and as adults, and we've examined how Jesus and the early church modeled discipleship for all ages.

If these five elements are necessary for our spiritual formation, how present are they in our ongoing journey to become more like Jesus today?

Time: How much time does the average Christian in the West spend in habitual, intimate community relationships designed to foster their growth to be more like Jesus? Perhaps one hour per week, or maybe two to five hours? How does that amount of time compare with the time required for our spiritual formation as young toddlers or what Jesus modeled with His disciples?

Habit: What habits are we as Christians engaging in that routinely draw us to Jesus? We attend a weekly church service and maybe a small group meeting once every two weeks or so. We have some prayer time with family or a close group of friends. What about Jesus's habit of perpetually looking into people's hearts and having those tough conversations or looking for ways to restore people? Are those habits of the average Christian?

Intimacy: How vulnerable, real, and confessional is the average American Christian in his or her circle of close friends? Paul was uncomfortably upfront about his past sins and his struggle to live in the two kingdoms, yet he was confident enough to encourage some of his students to follow his pattern of life if they wanted to follow Jesus. Do we regularly experience that type of intimacy in our Christian churches?

Community: Does the average American Christian have a close-knit, committed, long-standing, predictable group of believers in their lives who purposefully grow together to become like Jesus? Does the modern church cultivate this type of community? How does that get accomplished in large and mega-churches? Do small groups qualify as intentional, biblical communities? Can we cultivate a Christian community when we meet once every two weeks for a few hours and take the summers off?

Instruction: Western Christians do not lack biblical instruction. Book studies, apologetics, exegetical studies, topical studies, testimonies, Gospel presentations—never in history has a society had access to Christian instruction as we do. Yet, is this instruction self-directed, isolated, and scattershot? Or is it intentionally progressive, repetitious, and increasingly complex, moving a person to deeper and deeper spiritual things? Is it done *within* community, where doubts, dissent, and constructive debate are welcomed?

A Formation Gap Example

If becoming more like Jesus involves us embracing and embodying these five elements, is this the expectation and purpose of our modern church institutions today? Should we expect to be discipled in our current Christian institutions?

A church experience that my wife and I went through exemplifies the Formation Gap.

Jessica and I attended a standard American non-denominational church. The population of people attending weekend worship was growing, and church leadership asserted that the growth was a sign of a movement of God.

It's a typical church in that it holds a weekly service, has a small group effort, and offers a few programs for people who are grieving or struggling with addiction. The church has a youth group and a young adult program. They faithfully preach the Word.

However, we had no expectation of being discipled there. That's because the church doesn't display an understanding of biblical discipleship, and it lacks at least three of the five elements of spiritual formation.

Though the role of a pastor is often referred to as a "shepherd," we met the senior pastor one time. He had no idea who I was, though our family had volunteered and served in various capacities. That wasn't his fault; there are far too many people in the congregation for him to get to know and personally shepherd. He has publicly mourned that fact from the pulpit, but that didn't stop the church from a recent multi-million-dollar infrastructure expansion campaign.

He often referred to himself as "our pastor," though that didn't make sense if we consider the pastor as a shepherd. A shepherd knows his sheep, and the sheep know the shepherd's voice. Functionally, for most of the congregation, this senior pastor is simply the weekly Bible teacher or perhaps the "Senior Instructor."

Like most growing, larger churches, the Idea of "discipleship" is basically outsourced to small groups. They acknowledge the weekend service is primarily about worship in song and preaching. "Real community," we've been told, is found in small groups. However, the small group ministry involves virtually no training, nor is it connected to the pastoral staff or their instructional plan. In essence, the church just wants people to meet in homes for fellowship and has no purpose or vision beyond that.

So, while this church certainly embodies a commitment to biblical orthodoxy and provides a weekly half-hour biblically sound monologue, there is no expectation of "time" beyond that. Though the church is growing, it continually struggles to recruit volunteers for its expanding programs. The church expects little time investment from its congregation, so the congregation responds in kind.

The church provides no education or training on spiritual habits, be it prayer, silence, solitude, celebration, fasting, meditation, or others.

There is little opportunity to form a community during the weekend service. It's a multi-service environment, so the worship times are carefully calculated, and people are shuttled in and out in order to make room for the next service. Again, community is supposed to occur in small groups.

Jessica and I voluntarily led one of these groups for a year—the attendance was spotty. Because the church sets no expectation for discipleship, our small group had little expectation to attend unless it was convenient for them to do so.

Intimacy requires community. In the case of this church, the best examples of "intimacy in community" are its ministries for hurting people and people struggling with addiction or grief. Also (as is common in modern churches), ministries for kids and youth tend to cultivate a stronger community. However, those communities tend to have deeper commitments to time, specifically designed instruction, and habits.

This type of church experience may be foreign to you, or you may be nodding in familiar agreement. Keep in mind that ministry is certainly happening at churches such as this. People are being instructed, helped, and introduced to Jesus.

However, this particular church's lack of attention to genuine discipleship was summed up by the senior pastor during a sermon some years ago. "The primary purpose of the church," he announced, "is evangelism. I know the Great Commission tells us that we are to make disciples, but you can't have a disciple without a convert."

He is amiss on both points. The primary purpose of the church is not to make converts. Plus, we'd have far more genuine converts if we were far more intentional about making disciples.

However, his honest statement explains the philosophy and programs of this church. The church's purpose is to introduce as many people as possible to Jesus; thus, the focus is on weekend service attendees and the constant pressure to build more physical infrastructure. The overwhelming majority of time, money, and resources are poured into the setup and execution of the weekend services because that's where most people hear about Jesus. This church's primary objective is to "go wide, not deep."

To the best of my knowledge, there is no effort to train congregants on being a disciple or making disciples, though there is some expectation of evangelism (as it's commonly defined).

The church does not teach or train in the kingdom, and it provides little opportunity for people to explore their own stories as a means of Deep Discipleship. Its worship service and small group effort embody one to two elements of formation.

And, whether it's aware of this or not, the church assumes self-directed discipleship for the vast majority of its congregation. This particular church is not interested in Deep Discipleship; it is interested in making converts and helping a minority of adults struggling with addiction and grief, which is certainly admirable.

Thus, most of the congregation lives in the Formation Gap.

The Formation Gap and Neuroscience

Before we explore how we resolve these Three Primary Problems and dive into Deep Discipleship together, let's pause to consider one other downstream harm caused by the Formation Gap in conjunction with the Discipleship Dilemma—the minimization of your own story.

Let's return to two quotes from John Calvin and A. W. Tozer. Calvin wrote,

---

> We cannot expect to know God fully if we are not willing to know ourselves, for one depends on the other.

And Tozer provokingly commented:

> That our idea of God corresponds as nearly as possible to the true being of God is of immense importance to us. Compared with our actual thoughts about Him, our creedal statements are of little consequence. Our real idea of God may lie buried under the rubbish of conventional religious notions and may require an intelligent and vigorous search before it is finally unearthed and exposed for what it is. Only after an ordeal of painful self-probing are we likely to discover what we actually believe about God.[5]

Both comments underscore an essential part of our journey to become more like Jesus: understanding our own hearts and stories. Unfortunately, exploring how our hearts were formed, what Ideas and desires power us, and how they impact us today are areas rarely contemplated in today's environment.

As Christians, we recognize that, in our current age, relational trauma is all too common. We cannot consider Deep Discipleship without considering broken hearts, broken minds, and broken bodies. Too many of our Christian brothers and sisters, not to mention our friends outside the church, are the walking wounded.

Bessel van der Kolk is considered one of the pioneers and innovative leaders in the treatment of post-traumatic stress disorder (PTSD), and he wrote a comprehensive book called *The Body Keeps the Score*.

He opens his book with these words:

> One does not have to be a combat soldier, or visit a refugee camp in Syria, or the Congo to encounter trauma. Trauma happens to us, our friends, our families, and our neighbors. Research by the Center for Disease Control and Prevention has shown that one in five Americans was sexually molested as a child; one in four was beaten by a parent to the point of a mark being left on their body; and one in three couples engages in physical violence. A quarter of us grew up with alcoholic relatives, and one out of eight witnessed their mother being beaten or hit.[6]

We often hear trauma referred to as "Big T" or "little t." "Big T" traumas are some of what van der Kolk just listed: war, sexual abuse, physical abuse, horrible accidents, and sudden deaths of loved ones.

"Little t" traumas are highly distressing events that affect individuals on a personal level but don't fall into the "Big T" category. Examples of "little t" trauma include non-life-threatening injuries, emotional abuse, death of a pet, bullying or harassment, and loss of significant relationships.[7]

Events such as betrayal, divorce (whether you're the spouse or the child), or emotional and physical abandonment cause trauma and can be "Big T" or "little t," depending on the circumstances.

The point is, we've all been victims of trauma, whether it's "Big T" or "little t." Christians tend to minimize "little t" trauma, even though the Bible is clear that suffering is part of the human experience, so it's part of everyone's discipleship story.

For many Christians, exploring or even talking about "little t" trauma in the context of their spiritual formation and story supposedly indicates a lack of faith, a lack of perseverance, or weakness.

However, van der Kolk goes on to explain how trauma results in the "loss of self," something we have already identified discipleship is designed to recover.

The Importance of "Know Thyself"

One of van der Kolk's teachers said,

> "Most human suffering is related to love and loss and... the job of therapists is to help people 'acknowledge, experience, and bear' the reality of life—with all its pleasures and heartbreak. The greatest sources of our suffering are the lies we tell ourselves... people can never get better without knowing what they know and feeling what they feel."[8]

"The greatest sources of our suffering are the lies we tell ourselves." Instead of pressing into our suffering, instead of inviting and allowing others to extend compassion (which literally means "with suffering"), we cope. And we lie to ourselves, and the lies eventually become truth to us. And we "lose ourselves" in the process.

This is why practicing Heartview, being in a close community with other sojourners, and engaging in appropriate relational intimacy are so vital to our journey to become more like Jesus. We may lie to ourselves, but our hearts have a way of expressing reality whether we want them to or not. However, we need the Holy Spirit and a community of people who love us to help us translate the messages our hearts are sending.

Later in the book, van der Kolk breaks down the various parts of the brain and explains how a person must engage their story in order to return to wholeness:

> Most of our conscious brain is dedicated to focusing on the outside world: getting along with others and making plans for the future. However, that does not help us manage ourselves. Neuroscience research shows that the only way we can change the way we feel is by becoming aware of our inner experience and learning to befriend what is going on inside ourselves.[9]

Theologians talk about the inner self, the inner experience, and the inner man with some frequency. To some of our modern evangelical ears, exploring our "inner person" sounds like New Age nonsense. But to some of the greatest Christian minds of the last 2,000 years, exploring our inner person is an accepted and necessary aspect of a practice called "contemplation." We contemplate and dwell on God and His character, and we search our hearts... not because we're trying to become God or find our salvation in ourselves, but because we desire to grow to think, act, and love the way Jesus does.

It's fashionable in Christian circles today to downplay the suffering in our stories and compare it to others who have suffered more. We'll always find someone who has suffered more—it supposedly makes us feel better to find such a person.

In *Man's Search for Meaning*, though, Viktor Frankl wrote:

> A man's suffering is similar to the behavior of a gas. If a certain quantity of gas is pumped into an empty chamber, it will fill the chamber completely and evenly, no matter how big the chamber is. Thus suffering completely fills the human soul and conscious mind, no matter whether the suffering is great or little. Therefore the "size" of human suffering is absolutely relative.[10]

Pain is like a gas. It doesn't matter how much of it there is; it fills the room.

Therefore, we all experience suffering to one degree or another, and it serves little purpose to minimize or ignore it. How we choose to respond to our suffering has a tremendous impact on our discipleship.

If we accept that an essential part of discipleship is exploring who we are with our King, then we should ask ourselves: are we "befriending" our inner experience, our stories of hurt and trauma? Or do we ignore it, cope with it, or, as is so often the case today, use our religion to "duck and cover" from it?

Curt Thompson sums this thought up nicely: "Christian anthropology reveals, perhaps somewhat counterintuitively, that **the depth and intensity of our desire for and unity with God directly and proportionately mirror the degree to which we become the truest versions of our individual selves**."[11]

Half-brained Churches, Whole-brained People

Engaging our story in community, including our hopes and our hurts, our joys, and our sufferings, is an essential piece of the process by which we become more like Jesus.

However, we are generally poor at discovering our stories by ourselves. We are excellent liars, even to ourselves. We need God and trusted, safe friends who are willing to enter into our stories with us.

As we've explored, this is not the modern Idea of discipleship. We go to church, worship through music, hear the sermon, go home, and then proceed to "self-direct" our own spiritual formation.

But isn't the church the place where we should enter into immersive communities that are specifically designed to help us be formed into the likeness of Jesus by getting to know Him and ourselves?

Another neuroscientist, Dr. Jim Wilder, wrote a book with Pastor Michel Hendricks called *The Other Half of Church*. They write:

> We used the phrase "spiritual formation" which is a fancy way of talking about how we become more like Jesus in our daily lives. We react to life like He does. We value what He values. We treat people the way He treats people. It is the process of "putting on the character of Christ." We all agree that this was the central task of the church. We also agree that the church was mostly failing at this task.[12]

They go on to assert that modern Christianity is largely a left-brained effort. The left brain handles things like conscious thought, speech, strategies, problem-solving, and logic.

However, neuroscience has revealed that the *right brain* is bigger, faster, and has more horsepower. The right brain handles things like individual and group identity, emotional attachment to others, how we assess our surroundings, and relational attachments.[13]

The authors then conclude the modern church may be catering to the wrong side of the brain.

> ...our right brain governs the whole range of relational life: who we love, our emotional reactions to our surroundings, our ability to calm ourselves, and our identity, both as individuals and as a community. The right side manages our strongest relational connections (both to people and to God) and our experience of emotional connectedness to others. And character formation... Character formation, which is a primary responsibility of the church, is governed by the right brain, not the left brain.[14]

In other words, our spiritual formation, scientifically speaking, is more about individual and group identity, community, emotional attachment, attunement, and vulnerability than thoughts, speech, and rational logic.

They continue, "...our right brain depends on relational input to form our character. Much of the processing is nonverbal and preconscious."[15]

They aren't arguing that teaching, Bible studies, doctrine, worship experiences, apologetics, and preaching are bad. They're saying that, as a means of spiritual formation, those things are dramatically incomplete. Christian communities should be "whole-brained."

Modern neuroscience confirms the model of discipleship that Jesus and the early disciples modeled. We are formed into the likeness of Jesus more through our experiences, relationships, and vulnerability than through the areas the West currently emphasizes: teaching and intermittent spiritual events. In other words, we are best formed in intentional groups, which focus on time, habits, community, intimacy, and instruction.

Our understanding of our purpose in the kingdom, our exploration of our stories, and our journey into Deep Discipleship are best accomplished in specific communities designed around the same five elements we experience in virtually any formative environment.

Hopefully, we are already part of these types of communities in our church or some other format. However, because so many of us live in the Formation Gap, Soil & Roots went back to the New Testament and developed a simple way to replicate the types of formative communities Jesus and His early followers established.

We call them Greenhouses.

Chapter 9 Cumulative Key Takeaways

1. A potential solution to the Great Omission is a journey into Deep Discipleship, the intentional exploration of the

unconscious Ideas and desires that power and govern us.

2. However, in our current era, discipleship is hampered by Ideas that have formed the basis of three systemic and harmful cultural frameworks: the Forgotten Kingdom, the Discipleship Dilemma, and the Formation Gap.
3. We're struggling to comprehend and embrace Jesus as the King of a growing kingdom. We also struggle to move forward in our spiritual formation because doing so requires us to understand our own stories.
4. The lack of genuine discipleship is further compounded by the fact many of us do not have access to communities specifically designed to form us to be more like Jesus. Spiritual formation is best experienced in groups that embrace all five elements of formation: time, habit, community, intimacy, and instruction.

---

1. Charlie Baber, "Becoming Who We Are," *United Methodist Insight: Discerning God's Will for the Future*, accessed October 30, 2023, https://um-insight.net/perspectives/becoming-who-we-are/.
2. "Church And Religious Charitable Giving Statistics," *NP Source*, accessed October 30, 2023, https://nonprofitssource.com/online-giving-statistics/church-giving/.
3. Coleman, R. *Master Plan of Discipleship* (p. 59). Revell.
4. Willard, D., & Johnson, J. (2006). *Renovation of the Heart in Daily Practice: Experiments in Spiritual Transformation* (pp. 68–69). NavPress.
5. Willard, D. (2002). *Renovation of the Heart: Putting on the Character of Christ* (p. 100). NavPress.
6. Van der Kolk, B. (2014). *The Body Keeps the Score: Brain, Mind, and Body in the Healing of Trauma* (p. 1). Penguin Books.
7. Journey Pure Staff, "Big 'T' and little 't' Trauma," *JourneyPure: At the River*, accessed October 30, 2023, https://journeypureriver.com/big-t-little-t-trauma/.
8. Van der Kolk. *The Body Keeps the Score*, pp. 26–27. Penguin Books.
9. Van der Kolk. *The Body Keeps the Score*, p. 208. Penguin Books
10. Frankl, V. (1992). *Man's Search for Meaning* (p. 55). Beacon Press.
11. Thompson, C. (2021). *The Soul of Desire: Discovering the Neuroscience of Longing, Beauty, and Community* (p. 11). InterVarsity Press. Emphasis mine.
12. Wilder, J., & Hendrick, M. (2020). *The Other Half of Church: Christian Community, Brain Science, and Overcoming Spiritual Stagnation* (p. 14). Moody Publishers.
13. Wilder & Hendricks. *The Other Half of Church* (pp. 20–21). Moody.
14. Wilder & Hendricks. *The Other Half of Church* (p. 22). Moody.
15. Wilder & Hendricks. *The Other Half of Church* (p. 28). Moody.

Part Three
The Greenhouse Movement

Our Greenhouse and the *Soil & Roots* podcast have changed my entire paradigm of what discipleship is and how I grow to become more like Jesus.

—Anonymous Greenhouse Participant

Ten
What Is A Greenhouse?

We now turn our attention to the best news of the book: the Great Omission and the current Three Primary Problems can be resolved. We don't need to continue to experience this disconnection with God, others, ourselves, and creation and culture. We don't have to stay stuck in Stages 1, 2, and 3 of our spiritual journeys. We no longer need to wonder if there is more to the Christian life.

We simply recapture Deep Discipleship as Jesus and the disciples originally modeled through forming and supporting small communities specifically designed for our spiritual formation. And this is being done in conjunction with current church institutions, structures, and traditions. This is not a call for tearing down time-honored, effective institutional religious efforts. This is a call for reforming and restoring Deep Discipleship in the context of the modern era.

On the surface, it may appear daunting to consider how to re-introduce all five formative elements into our current lifestyle and church experience. How do we, together with God and others, restore New Testament discipleship? How do we resolve the Great Omission and the Three Primary Problems?

One solution is to form intentional, small, five-element

communities that purpose together to become more like Jesus. At Soil & Roots, we call these special, specific communities "Greenhouses."

If our hearts are like roots, and the soil in which our roots are planted represents the core Ideas and desires that form us, then (sticking with an agricultural theme) the communities in which those Ideas are transformed and nourished are essentially "greenhouses." A Greenhouse is a small group of committed sojourners who purposefully restore New Testament discipleship and intentionally resolve and reverse the Three Primary Problems.

- A Greenhouse explores and contemplates the Gospel of the Kingdom, thus resolving the Forgotten Kingdom.
- A Greenhouse embraces and accepts that spiritual formation involves knowing Jesus and His story and ourselves and our personal stories. It gives space for both to be explored. This resolves the Discipleship Dilemma.
- A Greenhouse embodies all five elements of formation, thus resolving the Formation Gap.

Our Greenhouse has become a primary community for me. We text each other throughout the week, we naturally pray for each other. We know what's going on in each other's lives. It's the type of group I needed... but didn't know I needed.

—Anonymous Greenhouse Participant

Practically, here is how a Greenhouse works.

The Greenhouse Gatherings

> But Christians have forgotten that the ministry of listening has been committed to them by Him who is Himself the great listener and whose work they should share. We should listen with the ears of God that we may speak the Word of God.
>
> —Dietrich Bonhoeffer[1]

Because a Greenhouse embodies all five elements (time, habit, community, intimacy, instruction), the gatherings and rhythms provided below are likely to differ from your church, small group, or Bible study. To be clear, Soil & Roots firmly and fully supports and endorses institutional churches, para-church organizations, and all efforts to make disciples and spread the Gospel of the Kingdom. At the same time, the Formation Gap is a pressing concern in the West.

Another way to view this challenge is through the lens of the book noted in Chapter 1, *The Critical Journey*.[2] The authors suggest there are six stages to our journey to become more like Jesus:

1. Recognition of God
2. The Life of Discipleship (renamed "The Life of Learning" for this book)
3. The Productive Life
4. The Journey Inward (including the Wall)
5. The Journey Outward
6. A Life of Love

If the authors' assessment of modern church institutions is accurate, in that most churches are structured and concerned primarily with the first three stages, a Greenhouse is a place to explore all six, with particular attention to the last three, including the Wall.

Thus, people who don't know Jesus or who are in the early stages are encouraged to become a part of a Greenhouse, as well as those at later stages. As you'll see, the gatherings and rhythms allow people at any phase of their journey to participate.

Greenhouse Basics

A Greenhouse is a group of four to twelve people who gather twice per week, in person if possible. Each gathering is 90 minutes long, and Soil & Roots provides a framework for each session.

Ideally, Greenhouses are formed around people who are already in a relationship, be it through a family, hobby, church, geography, friendships, work, or other existing connections. This isn't a must, though it helps to grow deeper in Christ with people with whom you already "do life."

The focus of a Greenhouse is to form genuine, mature disciples in small, committed, kingdom-centric communities. We do that by growing in our experience with Jesus while we discern our own hearts and stories. Greenhouses are more about listening to God, others, and our own hearts compared to other models of teaching and response.

Roles

A Greenhouse includes three roles: Facilitator, Host, and Participant. The facilitator leads and administrates the gatherings, the host coordinates the details of the group and opens their residence, workplace, church, or other location for the gatherings, and the participants are committed members of the community. The facilitator and host may be the same person, and the host is also a participant.

In the Soil & Roots ecosystem, facilitators must apply to form a Greenhouse. This simple process is designed to ensure facilitators embrace and align with the Statement of Faith and the core principles of Soil & Roots, have a passion for the kingdom and Deep Discipleship, and desire to hear and explore other people's stories.

A facilitator is not a teacher, so critical characteristics of this role include careful listening and the ability to gently guide conversation. Because a Greenhouse's "success" is deeply tied to the character, maturity, and listening skills of the facilitator, Soil & Roots provides ongoing training and community for those who choose to facilitate.

As noted, the host and participants may be at various stages in their spiritual formation or may not yet be apprenticing with Jesus.

I've always struggled with how I'm supposed to be a disciple. Our Greenhouse is helping me not only define it but also understand how to actually live it.

—Anonymous Greenhouse Participant

Gathering 1

Greenhouses feature four weekly "rhythms," two per gathering.

The two rhythms of the first weekly gathering are **Reflection** and **Exploration**.

A central theme of Soil & Roots is "less monologue, more dialogue." So, the facilitator's role is generally not to present materials and teach. It's to provide a forum for the Greenhouse to answer and raise questions, express doubts or confusion, and dig deep into the journey of spiritual formation in the kingdom.

The bulk of this gathering is for interactive, honest discussion and biblical exploration. Soil & Roots believes that teaching is best absorbed and is most transformative when it is wrestled with in a trusted group.

Gathering 1 Format

Opening (prayer, hymn or worship song, and segue): 10–15 minutes

Ask someone to open up the gathering in prayer. Then, if your Greenhouse has a person gifted in music and worship, consider a hymn or worship song. Then start the "segue," which is simply a chance for each person to share a short piece of personal or professional good news from the week. It serves as an icebreaker and a means to begin sharing. Sharing this piece of news should take no more than a minute or so per person.

Reflection: 20 minutes

This is an open time when participants may share questions, thoughts, concerns, doubts, disagreements, and affirmations of the previous week's gatherings.

The facilitator may choose to use the simple Reflection Questions below as a guide or lead the discussion as he/she sees fit. The point is to allow the Greenhouse to explore the previous week's discussions concerning their spiritual journey further.

Sample Reflection Questions:

- Has there been a verse, comment, theme, or point that has stood out to you from last week's four rhythms? Why do you think it has been on your mind or heart?
- Have any of your Ideas (unconscious assumptions or concepts) about your faith, life, or story been challenged or solidified because of last week's gatherings? If comfortable, please share how your understanding of Jesus's story or your own story is being impacted.
- Throughout the week, have you noticed God reminding or reinforcing something He brought into your heart from last week? Would you mind sharing how He did that?

Exploration: 40 minutes

Currently, the material for this portion of the gathering is the *Soil & Roots* podcast. The podcast is a purposefully designed journey that slowly and carefully draws the listener into a deep and rich experience of spiritual formation. It walks through the basics of spiritual formation, introduces the concept of "Ideas," and explores the Three Primary Problems and their solutions.

The podcast moves slowly and embodies the method of "repetitious and increasingly complex" instruction as part of the commitment to the Five Key Elements.

The group simply listens to (or reads) one episode per week prior to this gathering. Some Greenhouses opt to spend more than one week exploring each episode. The podcast is fairly dense, and the point is not to "get through it" as quickly as possible but rather to allow the group to fully discuss, debate, and vet the points they wish to explore.

All facilitators are provided with Exploration Questions along with relevant Bible passages for each episode. The facilitator guides a discussion using the provided materials.

To encourage transparent, honest, open discussion, the facilitator may include other questions and points that encourage deeper biblical study, observations from personal lives or the culture, or the sharing of parts of individual stories.

The objective for this portion is to transparently share about the episode and how it relates to the story of Jesus and our own stories. It is not to teach, lecture, judge, or even correct every perceived theological error. Doubt and dissent are welcomed, as are affirmation and requests for clarification.

Because many people don't have access to communities where they feel safe to share their confusions and concerns, a facilitator should carefully create an environment where that type of engagement is welcomed and honored.

Closing (administrative issues and closing prayer): 10 minutes

The facilitator and/or host may have specific topics to discuss, such as meal information for Gathering 2, holiday schedules, information on the next podcast episode, serving opportunities, etc. Then, the facilitator may ask someone to close in prayer (or pray themselves).

Gathering 2

The two rhythms of Gathering 2 are **Soul Care** and **Spiritual Habits.** This gathering is to be held (if possible) in conjunction with a shared meal (what we jokingly refer to as a "Gastro Greenhouse").

Gathering 2 focuses solely on the care and spiritual practices of the participants in the community.

In the 1700s, John Wesley adopted and promoted a mid-week, small gathering called the "Class Meeting." Its format was simple, and the key question asked each week was, "How is it with your soul?" Wesley was so convinced about the power and value of the Class Meeting that it was made mandatory in the Methodist church for many years.

Though Soul Care is defined in various ways, in Greenhouses, it refers to the state of our holistic relationship with God. We might ask, "How is our walk with Jesus?" or "How is our spiritual life this week?"

The intent is to open a free-flowing dialogue in our trusted communities about our journey of discipleship. As with Gathering 1, facilitators lead and guide an appropriate discussion with kindness, patience, and gentleness, understanding participants are at various places and stages in their spiritual journey. Some participants are, right now, experiencing a "dark night of the soul," and the Greenhouse may be their only place to allow others to suffer with them and to help them in and through their suffering.

Secondly, each Greenhouse discusses and decides on a spiritual discipline (or habit) that the group wishes to test and explore for a period of time. Each week, the Greenhouse will talk about the habit, how it's going, and what they are experiencing as they practice it. There is no master list of habits, though some commonly accepted disciplines are prayer, solitude, silence, confession, celebration, service, heart listening, and fasting. For more information or ideas, see Richard Foster's *Celebration of Discipline* or Dallas Willard's *Spirit of Disciplines.*

Though spiritual disciplines have been central to the life of Christians throughout church history, modern Christianity has largely lost the study and practice of these ancient habits. The Greenhouse is a place where we may recover what Christ modeled for us as we desire to become more like Him.

Gathering 2 Format

Opening (prayer, hymn or worship song, segue): 10–15 minutes

Soul care: 40 minutes

This portion of the gathering focuses on exploring our own hearts and stories while considering and embracing the heart of Jesus.

The facilitator may open the discussion with a simple question, such as:

- "How is your life with God?"
- "How is your walk with Jesus going?"
- "How's it going with your soul?"

The facilitator then leads a time of sharing, keeping the group focused on how each of us grows in Christ and the inward journey of exploring our own stories.

The facilitator should ensure that all parties who wish to share and contribute have the opportunity to do so. The Greenhouse should practice good listening, as well as provide encouragement, counsel, and guidance where appropriate and welcomed.

If the Greenhouse has worked through the podcast's Season 2 and has become comfortable with Heartview, the facilitator may opt to ask a question specific to our Eight Indicators, such as:

- "How has your thought life been this week?"
- "Did you make financial decisions this week that reflect the heart of Jesus?"
- "How are your emotions pointing you to what you truly desire?"
- "Are you relating to others the way Jesus relates to us?"

Spiritual habits: 20 minutes

Each Greenhouse will collaboratively discuss and decide to "practice" a spiritual habit for a period and talk openly about its impact. This may be something like "pray 15 minutes a day" or "spend ten minutes in silence and Scripture meditation three times per week." Or perhaps it may be to practice the habit of confession in an appropriate relationship.

Once the Greenhouse has decided on a habit it wishes to practice, each week, this time is allotted for the group to share their experiences, ask questions, raise concerns, and learn from one another's stories. As with all elements of the Greenhouse, the group leans on the Holy Spirit for guidance regarding which habit to practice and for how long.

Closing (administrative issues and closing prayer): 10 minutes

The facilitator and/or host may have specific topics to discuss, such as meal information, holiday schedules, information on the next podcast episode, serving opportunities, etc. Then, the facilitator may ask someone to close in prayer (or pray themselves).

Because eating together played such a key role in New Testament discipleship, Gathering 2 features a weekly meal together, and the rhythms are explored while eating.

There is much more information on how to form, facilitate, and grow Greenhouses on the Soil & Roots website, including a helpful FAQ.

Our Greenhouse isn't like anything else I've experienced. The podcast material isn't your typical Bible study, and the four rhythms impact us all throughout the week. When I talk about the Greenhouse to my friends, they often ask, "Oh, so it's like a small group or Bible study?" "No," I reply. "It's not like either of those. It's a Greenhouse. You just have to experience it to understand it.

—Anonymous Greenhouse Participant

The Greenhouse Ecosystem

If the format, roles, and rhythms of the Greenhouse gatherings appear simplistic, it's because they are. Four rhythms, three roles, two gatherings per week.

Yet, this simple approach to community formation intentionally embraces and embodies all five elements of our formation.

Time: Greenhouses very purposefully commit to becoming a "primary" group for those involved. Though our current lifestyle often forces us to be a part of multiple groups apart from our work relationships with limited time commitments in each (church congregation, small group, PTA, band boosters, volunteer groups, etc.), that type of disintegrated community lifestyle does not lend itself well to spiritual formation.

Greenhouses commit to gathering twice a week as a means of combating and resolving this community disintegration. The time commitment to the group is entirely purposeful and necessary for Deep Discipleship. Oftentimes, relationships are fostered outside of the weekly gatherings as well. Participants may gather on their own for separate meals, holiday gatherings, incidental conversations, and fellowship events.

Habits: Though the practice of spiritual disciplines has been somewhat lost in the modern age beyond vague obligations to prayer, perhaps fasting, and the rituals of Christian worship experiences, many of our Christian ancestors developed lives centered around various spiritual habits. Jesus modeled habits (many of which we didn't mention here), and subsequent disciples embraced the creativity of the Holy Spirit through the testing and practice of various disciplines.

In Greenhouses, the community prayerfully decides on a discipline or two to practice and grows together in the evaluation and improvement of that practice. The spiritual life of the Greenhouse is deepened and greatly enhanced by the collective embracing of these habits through that portion of Gathering 2.

Community: At Soil and Roots, we often refer to Greenhouses as "sitcom" communities. For decades, the situational comedy genre has featured show after show about small groups of people who lived together, worked together, suffered together, and experienced life in all of its ups and downs together. Comedies such as *Friends*, *Parks and Recreation*, *Cheers*, and even *Seinfeld* reflect a deep desire planted in the heart of every human being—to be a part of a committed, long-term, small group of people who accept us and love us despite our quirks, flaws, sins, and personality traits, a group that knows us, will be there for us, and can be relied on.

This type of "sitcom" community was the norm in times past. With the birth of the Industrial Revolution, mass transportation, transient lifestyles, and technological advances, this type of community has largely disappeared in many parts of the world. This is what makes the sitcom so attractive to so many viewers—we long for what they have. This is the type of community a Greenhouse fosters and intentionally cultivates.

Intimacy: If our primary Christian experience is a weekend worship service, a Bible study, and private devotional time, we are presented with few "sanctioned" times to be ourselves, to open our hearts, and to explore our stories with other trusted friends. We have few places to vent our anger, confess our shortcomings, and share our inner joys without fear of being shunned or abandoned. Unless we are part of various helpful recovery groups (AA, Celebrate Recovery), which intentionally allow and encourage self-contemplation and story exploration, many people have no consistent experience where they are encouraged to dig beneath the surface to explore the Ideas and desires that govern their hearts.

True relational intimacy requires time, trust, and an inviting but non-critical environment. This is the culture and atmosphere of a Greenhouse in all four of its rhythms.

Instruction: Because this is the commonly accepted (and unconsciously assumed) catalyst of discipleship, most Westerners are comfortable with this element.

However, Greenhouses take an interactive, progressively deepening approach to instruction. The raw material for the Exploration rhythm (the *Soil & Roots* podcast) is designed as a "repetitious, increasingly complex" journey into Deep Discipleship. Human beings typically learn well through repeated principles that grow into more complex concepts over time, and the podcast embodies that philosophy.

Unlike many traditional learning environments (where we are presented information in a monologue or through directed teaching), Greenhouses are exploratory communities in that they reflect a "less monologue, more dialogue" philosophy. Doubts, dissent, and constructive debate are welcomed and encouraged, as Soil & Roots maintains that learning is best embraced and absorbed when openly discussed and worked through as a group. This is reflected in both the Reflection and Exploration rhythms in Gathering 1.

There are three models of Greenhouses: church, para-church, and mixed. The "church" model sits within the existing framework of a local church. It's a "program" of a specific church body. The para-church model has participants from various churches. This model looks like the popular Bible Study Fellowship effort.[3] The mixed model features people from one church, various churches, or no church. In some cases, people are not attending a local church for various reasons (they can't find one, they've been victims of spiritual abuse, health reasons, etc.); however, they wish to be a part of a discipleship community. In other cases, people who don't yet know Jesus are invited and wish to be part of a Greenhouse. Soil & Roots helps to form and support all three models.

Soil & Roots provides more information on Greenhouses and how to start and support them on our website, www.soilandroots.org.

When I first learned that Greenhouses gather twice a week, I thought that was nuts. Who has time to get together that often? Now I know—people who yearn for Jesus, desire to experience deep community, and are desperate to become more like Him have time to meet twice a week. Now, I wouldn't have it any other way.

—Anonymous Greenhouse Participant

A Beginning

We started our journey in the introduction with the premise that many people who wish to follow Jesus today experience a conscious or unconscious disconnection from their faith. The promises of Scripture, be it the abundant life, being provided what we pray for, relief from anxiety and fear, a sense our lives should be characterized by doing the things Jesus did, or a willingness to suffer and sacrifice with others, appear more aspirational and future-bound than descriptions of our lives at present.

In short, we experience the "Great Omission." We miss the wonderful opportunity to experience the later stages of discipleship. And we realize that the Great Omission is wreaking havoc not only on ourselves, but on families, communities, cities, and even nations.

Yet we sense the Christian life *is* deeper and richer than what we normally experience. Our hearts long for what we've termed Deep Discipleship—an exploration of the hidden Ideas and desires that form us, our churches, and our culture. This seems to be the realm where Jesus lived and operated, and we genuinely desire to become more like Him.

Our church rituals and service opportunities are wonderful and formative experiences, though they may not lead to the deeper heart formation we long for if we don't engage in the difficult work of plumbing the depths of our hearts. As John Calvin, A. W. Tozer, Dallas Willard, and so many other thinkers and philosophers have proposed, these deep Ideas and desires in our hearts are often far removed from our intellectual belief system.

Few of us wish to go into those depths to investigate what we might find, but for those who do, Deep Discipleship awaits. We do learn to love as Jesus loves, to desire what He desires, and to relate as He relates. Our Ideas and desires are transformed into His Ideas and desires.

The human heart generally requires certain elements in order to experience this type of deep formation. Unfortunately, the modern Christian experience is not well acquainted with these five elements, and our lifestyles often work against them. This is where we who desperately long for the transformative Christian life must now turn our attention and our hearts. Surely, not just for ourselves, but for the goodness and well-being of our spouses, our children, our families, our communities, and our culture.

The Ideas of the kingdom of darkness distort, destroy, disintegrate, and eventually lead to death. This is true in all four of our relationships: with God, others, ourselves, and creation and culture.

The Ideas of the kingdom of light, however, point us back to the

Garden of Eden (and the eventual "better Eden," the new heaven and the new earth), which is why so many of Jesus's Ideas start with the prefix "re": restore, renew, redeem, rescue, recreate, reconcile, resurrect.

The path of a deep disciple, therefore, is one of identifying deadly dark Ideas in our relationships with God, others, ourselves, and creation and doing what Jesus did—replacing them with Ideas of restoration and renewal.

If we consciously or unconsciously embrace Ideas of darkness, we withdraw, we concede, we fear, we separate. As our hearts are formed more and more through Ideas of light, we advance, we conquer, we inspire, we re-integrate, we unify. We do what Jesus did—take the things the darkness has broken and put them back together. Though His path is costly, it is the path of a deep disciple.

These hidden, unconscious, governing, powerful Ideas do need to be uncovered, discerned, and transformed, starting in our own hearts. And then may we, like Jesus, take to the mission of uncovering them in all corners of His world, sacrificially and lovingly transforming dark Ideas to light, as we carry out the Great Commandment to love God, our neighbors, and ourselves as we steward and cultivate the earth on behalf of our King.

> A plan in the heart of a man is like deep water, but a man of understanding draws it out.[4]
>
> Watch over your heart with all diligence, for from it flow the springs of life.[5]

Chapter 10 Cumulative Key Takeaways

1. The Great Omission and the Three Primary Problems can be resolved by restoring the types of discipleship communities Jesus and the disciples modeled. And they can be restored in ways that honor and complement church institutions and the modern lifestyle.
2. Soil & Roots helps form and support these types of intentional communities. We call them Greenhouses.
3. Greenhouses are a means to help us reverse our disconnectedness from God, others, ourselves, creation, and culture and to dive into the deeper end of discipleship (Stages 4, 5, and 6 and the Wall).
4. Greenhouses meet twice a week and practice four simple "rhythms": Reflection, Exploration, Soul Care, and Spiritual Habits. The intentionality and cadence of the gatherings provide integration, connectedness, and consistency in our journey to become more like Jesus.

---

1. Chad Hill, "What Bonhoeffer Says About Listening," *CAM: Coach Approach Ministries*, accessed October 30, 2023, https://coachapproachministries.org/what-bonhoeffer-says-about-listening/.
2. Hagberg, J., & Guelich, R. (2005). *The Critical Journey: Stages in the Life of Faith.* Sheffield Publishing Company.
3. See Bible Study Fellowship for more information at https://www.bsfinternational.org/.
4. Proverbs 20:5
5. Proverbs 4:23

Terms And Definitions

Ideas: Conclusions, assumptions, and principles in which our hearts are rooted, but of which we are generally unaware. Ideas are not so much intellectual conclusions as they are deep, experienced realities. Ideas power and govern individuals, communities, cultures, and nations.

Disciple: An apprentice of Jesus who purposes to become more like Him.

Deep Discipleship: The ongoing journey of exploring and transforming the Ideas and desires that form us, the church, and the culture for the purpose of becoming more like Jesus.

Self-directed Discipleship: The common experience of a Western Christian, whereby their spiritual formation is (usually unconsciously) guided by themselves. This journey normally lacks a clear vision, path, or context, and results in "malformation," stunted progress, or a somewhat aimless meandering through the Christian life.

The Four Relationships: All human beings exist in four relationship categories: with God, with others, with ourselves, and with creation and culture. At Soil and Roots, we consider culture as the downstream derivative of creation (i.e., how human beings take creation's raw material and form it for our use).

The Seven Mountains of Culture: A simple way to describe and categorize areas of human interaction with ourselves in the created order: Family, Business, Church, Arts & Entertainment, Government, Media, and Education.

The Three Primary Problems: Widespread, powerful, disintegrating challenges currently plaguing the West. Though the problems pertain to the church, they impact all four of our relationships: with God, others, ourselves, and creation.

- **The Forgotten Kingdom:** The fact that Western Christianity has neglected the concept and cosmic nature of the Kingdom of God, having diminished its breadth and scope to personal relationships with Jesus.
- **The Discipleship Dilemma:** To become more like Jesus, it is essential we know Him and ourselves. Not only do we struggle to comprehend Jesus as King, but we oftentimes are also not invited or encouraged to understand our own stories as a means of growing to be more like Jesus.
- **The Formation Gap:** The fact that many apprentices of Jesus do not have access to communities specifically designed to form us more like Jesus. Yet virtually every other human growth environment purposefully embodies the five key elements.

The Five Key Elements of Spiritual Formation: Various factors common to the human experience that have tremendous influence on how Ideas are formed in our hearts. They are: time, habit, community, intimacy, and instruction.

Heartview: The ongoing habit of cooperating with God and trusted friends to explore the hidden Ideas in our hearts. This process involves identifying various "indicators" common to our human nature and asking "why" these indicators are present. Heartview normally involves exploring personal story, relationships, influences, and experiences.

The Eight Indicators: Ideas and desires in the human heart may be identified and evaluated by exploring patterns in our thoughts, emotions, behaviors, relationships, health, words, and use of time and money.

Christian Fatalism: The prominent modern, Western Idea in the hearts of many Christians that the earth is facing an inevitable demise, be it annihilation or various forms of worldwide destruction, suffering, and death, prior to Christ's consummation of the Kingdom. Soil and Roots explores Christian fatalism not so much from the Scriptural interpretations that lead to it, but from the underlying Ideas that both cause and result from it.

The Reductionist Gospel: A theological term that is most often associated with the modern-day assumption of "the Gospel." Whereas the Gospel of the Kingdom is the good news of Jesus incepting and growing a worldwide, restorative reality, the Reductionist Gospel (also known as the Gospel of Salvation) focuses solely on the good news of Christ restoring individuals to God.

Greenhouse: A specific type of community formed and supported by Soil and Roots that embodies and embraces all five elements of spiritual formation. A group of 4-12 people gathers twice a week to engage in four specific rhythms: Reflection, Exploration, Soul Care, and Spiritual Habits. The purpose of these communities is to journey together to become more like Jesus.

About The Author

Brian Fisher is the founder of Soil & Roots, an organization committed to cultivating deep discipleship. Soil & Roots helps form and support small groups of people who gather regularly to become more like Jesus, restoring the New Testament model of community-based spiritual formation.

Brian spent his early career in various executive roles in both for-profit companies and non-profit Christian ministries. He has spoken around the country on issues such as cultural engagement, media, bioethics, and apologetics, and is the author of four previous books and various published articles. He is also a Colson Fellow, having completed the Colson Center's extensive training program on Christian worldview, and is the primary host of the *Soil & Roots* podcast.

Brian lives with his wife, Jessica, in the Dallas area and they have two young adult sons.

Made in the USA
Columbia, SC
20 December 2024